HOW TO BE A BETTER FRIEND

How To Be Unbelievably Friendly

CHRIS STOREY

KINGSWAY PUBLICATIONS
EASTBOURNE

ISBN 0 85476 830 0

Published by
KINGSWAY PUBLICATIONS
Lottbridge Drove, Eastbourne, BN23 6NT, England.
E-mail: books@kingsway.co.uk

Designed and produced for the publishers by
Bookprint Creative Services, P.O. Box 827, BN21 3YJ, England.
Printed in Great Britain.

Contents

Introduction   7

Section One: To Mobility . . . and Beyond!

1. 'If You're Sitting Comfortably . . .'   15
2. New Genes   21
3. To Mobility . . . and Beyond!   27
4. Eat Your Greens!   31
5. 'A Heart for the Lost'?   35
6. The Key to Successful Enthusiasm   41
7. A Trip Around the Bay   47
8. Anoraks Anonymous   55
9. Look How Far You've Come!   61
10. 'I'll Get My Coat!'   65
11. Out of the Blue   71
12. 'A Friend of Sinners'?   79

Section Two: Running to Win

13. What Is the Gospel? (Part 1)   93
14. What Is the Gospel? (Part 2)   103
15. What Is the Gospel? (Part 3)   115

6   CONTENTS

16. The Sovereignty of God in Salvation   123
17. Leading Someone to Christ   133
18. Can You Hear Me?   141
19. Making the Most of Every Opportunity   157
20. The Promise Is for You   167
21. Into the Unknown   177

    Further Recommended Reading   187

Introduction

At 3.56 a.m. on 21st July 1969, Neil Armstrong became the first person to stand on the moon. On 1st June 1953, Edmund Hillary and Sherpa Tensing conquered Everest, the highest mountain in the world. On 14th December 1911, Roald Amundsen beat Captain Scott in the race to the South Pole. On 6th May 1954, Roger Bannister ran a mile in under four minutes (3 min: 59.4 sec:). On 30th July 1966, England beat West Germany 4–2 to win the World Cup. And at 12.05 p.m. on 26th January 1997, I prayed with my friend Geoff as he gave his life to Christ and was 'born again'.

Of all these events, only one sparked off a massive 'heaven-wide' celebration – and it wasn't anything to do with Hurst's third goal! Luke 15:7 tells us that heaven rejoices 'over one sinner who repents'. When people turn to Jesus – it's 'party time'. I don't know whether the angels were too bothered about the exploits of Neil, Edmund, Roald or Roger, but I do know that when Geoff turned his back on thirty-four years of living without God, they sat up and started celebrating.

There are many great things you can do with your life –

some may get you in the history books, others may not. It seems to me that the greatest thing any one of us can do is to help a friend come to Christ. Of all the things you can do, this one has eternal repercussions every time. It is more significant than being the first person to leave a footprint where no one has ever set foot before. It is of greater value and worth more praise than scoring the winning goal in a World Cup final. When heaven looks at those heroic men and women who have run the fastest, climbed the highest, swum the furthest and flown the longest, they pale in significance next to ordinary Christians who share their experience of Jesus with those who don't yet know him.

> ❛ It seems to me that the greatest thing any one of us can do is to help a friend come to Christ. ❜

Today, we find ourselves living in exciting times. Alpha courses are enabling more people than ever to look into the 'questions of life', to reason about the claims of Christ and to take up the opportunity to relate to the one who made those claims. In Britain, at least, there hasn't been a time like this for decades. But still, Christian friends say to me, 'I would love to bring someone to our Alpha course but I don't even know any unbelieving people. Where do I start?'

> ❛ There was a time when I thought that the only thing I could ever have in common with evangelists such as John Wesley or George Whitefield was to be dead too! ❜

Spending your life in leading people to Christ is a wonderful ideal, but there are many Christians who would say, 'I don't know whether I could lead *one* person to Christ, let alone a hundred!' I know I certainly felt this once. (There was a time when I thought that the only thing I could ever have in common with evangelists such as John Wesley or George Whitefield was to be dead too!)

Being not doing

Now I believe more strongly than ever that every Christian can have the joy of helping lost people find new life in Jesus Christ. Whether you are there, praying with your friend at the moment of their conversion, or whether you help them take just two or three steps closer to faith, both are equally worthy of a 'Well done!' from Jesus!

You may not think you can help people to become Christians at the moment, but the joy is that we can all do it. The secret lies in *being* something rather than *doing* something. People who are not Christians need a Christian friend who is not threatened by their non-Christian beliefs and doesn't see them as an evangelistic project. They need someone who is comfortable with being Christ-like in their company without being puritanical about their behaviour; they need someone they can experience Jesus through because he can be seen in their actions as well as their words. In short, unbelievers need a friend who *is* evangelistic, rather than someone who *does* evangelism. They need someone like you – or, someone like you can be!

Personal involvement

A person who believes in something accomplishes more than the person who just acts out of duty. That's why soldiers who volunteer for a mission are more desirable than 'pressed men'. Our mission, as 'soldiers of Christ', is to make disciples of all the nations. Whether we are pressed men or volunteers depends on whether we believe in the mission.

Years ago, a general would sit in an office miles away from the front line and give orders as to exactly how the troops were to fight (often with disastrous consequences). Many Christians feel that their experience of evangelism has been somewhat similar. They were told what to say and when to say it (often with the aid of a complicated diagram), with the result that the 'natural touch' was lost.

On the modern battlefield, an army is broken down into small units who are then given an objective. *How* they accomplish that objective is left up to them, for they are the ones who have to accomplish it! This approach has shown that people are willing to 'give' far more when they are personally more 'involved'.

Principles

If you are genuinely 'born again', you won't need much convincing about the rightness of the mission, but you may have a lot of hang-ups about how you can begin to show others all that Jesus has done for you and wants to do for them. I could tell you how I would try to lead your friends to Christ, but if you did it my way, they might run a mile, because you're not me. However, if I give you the principles I have found which have made me a better soldier, I won't win your friends to Christ, but I might help you to make your own plan as to how *you* will.

The aim of this book, therefore, is to give you some of the principles I have found helpful in causing me to *be* evangelistic rather than give you another evangelistic method to *do*. The chapters are designed to help you progress by stirring both your thinking and your actions. At the end of each, there are questions to ask yourself and practical steps to take as a result. The aim is to develop you as a person, not just to 'sharpen a tool'.

The first half of the book deals with the principles of becoming 'unbelievably friendly'. The second half deals with the content of the gospel. The reason it is this way round is because the 'content' of the gospel has the greatest effect when it travels on a 'track' of relationship. For years we have been told that the most 'successful' form of outreach is relational outreach – where you have spent time making a friend as well as 'preaching the gospel'. And in my experience, I've found this to be true.

You may find that going through this book with another Christian is of greater benefit than going through it on your own. You can discuss the issues raised and encourage one another as you both progress. Why not plan a time regularly – either each week or twice a month – to get together with a Christian friend and review how you are both doing as you go through each chapter?

Time and eternity

The time you invest in going through each chapter can produce lasting benefit and help you to become more evangelistic. Other people invest millions of pounds in doing stuff of no eternal value. Billions of dollars were spent to get Neil Armstrong on the moon and then the first thing he did was to mess up his pre-written 'speech'! (He was actually supposed to say,'This is one small step for *a* man, one giant leap for mankind'!) Will you invest, not money, but time in order to grow in doing stuff of eternal value?

I've never preached to packed auditoriums, and I haven't led thousands (or even hundreds) to Christ, but I have had the joy of leading a few more to salvation than most of my friends. I've written here about how I learned to do it, and I pray that this will be of use to you. If this book helps you to lead just one person to Christ in the future, then it will have accomplished all I hoped it would.

Chris Storey

SECTION ONE

To Mobility . . . and Beyond!

I

'If You're Sitting Comfortably . . .'

The first time I heard the gospel message after I had become a Christian, my heart skipped a beat! Have you ever heard anything more amazing, challenging, wonderful and inspiring in your life than the gospel? Every time I hear what Jesus did that first Easter I am moved. Even at times when I have been drifting or backsliding, the gospel of God reaches the parts other truths do not. I can never deny it; I don't just *believe* it is true, I *know* it is. There is something about the gospel of God that is in my soul as well as my intellect. It is not just my most treasured philosophy (if that's the right word to use), the gospel is alive within me!

I became a Christian when I was sixteen, after a number of months as a lapsed atheist. I never tried to be evangelistic, but I just kept finding myself in conversations about Jesus, or praying for people when they told me of needs in their lives. This, I learned, was called 'being a bold witness'. Friends and relatives became Christians around me – it was wonderful. 'How do you do it?' church friends asked. They, it seemed, did not have my 'courage and determination'. In

15

their opinion I had somehow acquired that elusive, 'grail-ish' object known as 'a heart for the lost'!

Normal or what?

Boldness? Courage? Determination? Heart for the lost? The terminology that I began to hear awakened me to a shocking truth: I was not a normal Christian! I was doing things no normal Christian would find easy, or enjoyable.

> **❝ I watched as grown men came close to tears at the thought of "open airs". ❞**

I began to feel uneasy, especially as I got more involved in the evangelistic events that the church organised. Few people seemed to like doing them much. Others braced themselves beforehand. I watched as grown men came close to tears at the thought of 'open airs'. Even elders, leading from the front, clutching tracts behind their backs (where they could not be spotted), stood in bus-stop queues, hoping to convince the 'raving evangelists' that they were talking to 'non-Christians', while simultaneously convincing the 'non-Christians' that they were actually waiting for the Number 51 and had nothing to do with the nutters singing 'God is good'.

Things were getting pretty tense! But fortunately I was running out of unbelieving friends. It didn't seem wise to make any new ones and I wanted to be normal, so I began to settle down to a life of getting stressed about the bi-monthly open airs and coming up with ever more ingenious ways of avoiding them altogether. Evangelism was doors and open airs. It was for masochists, ex-drug addicts or prisoners, people who had been bad enough to have a good testimony. I wanted to be a pastor!

Pastors loved the gospel, they read books about it. They studied the theology of it. They preached it. I liked pastors! The thing I liked the most about pastors though was they didn't have to '*do*' evangelism. What's more, people didn't think pastors were weird. Oh yes – I wanted to be a pastor! But God, it seems, had other plans.

It's only natural

At my Wednesday night housegroup one week, I sat waiting for the study topic to be announced. I was thoroughly committed to what I thought was a 'pastoral lifestyle'. I had been out to Marks & Spencer and bought a Fair Isle jumper, along with the regulation brown corduroys that were the hallmark of early 80s charismatic regalia. I had said 'hello' to everyone in the room at least twice . . . so far, so good! A leading role at holiday Bible weeks was already beckoning . . . Then the housegroup leader announced that for the next month we would be doing a series on evangelism. I can clearly remember thinking, 'Oh, grief, wake me up in a month's time!' I felt that I had moved on from all that, to 'more mature things'.

Part of the month's homework was to read a book that had something to do with evangelism. I have always loved reading about people's lives, especially those of notable Christians. The books about Jim Elliot and the other four missionaries martyred in South America during the 1950s had made a major impact on me when I was first saved. No other book (apart from the Bible) had inspired me more than

Jim Elliot's diary. No other book, that is, until the one I was about to stumble across.

To fulfil my duty and read a book on evangelism, I went along to my local Christian bookshop and began searching the shelves. I had heard about a man called Arthur Blessitt who carried a huge wooden cross around the world and spoke to people about Jesus. So when I came across his autobiography, *Arthur, A Pilgrim*, I thought I'd try reading it as my 'book for the month'. If nothing else, I thought it would be interesting to read about the different cultures he came across.

As I read, I began to 'feel my heart strangely warmed'. Something within me that I had successfully put to sleep, awoke. I read about a man who loved Jesus, who loved the gospel and who loved to share the message of the cross with anyone and everyone. But what hit me the most was that, for him, evangelism came naturally. It wasn't something he had laboured to graft onto his life, it was something he had *allowed* to grow out of his relationship with Jesus.

❛ the desire to tell other people about Jesus and to bring them to Christ is a *natural* desire in a Christian. ❜

Then it began to dawn on me: hadn't evangelism come naturally to me once as well? Hadn't I found that sharing my faith was something I did without thinking? Hadn't it been something which grew out of *my* relationship with Jesus too? I saw at that time what I believe wholeheartedly now, that the desire to tell other people about Jesus and to bring them to Christ is a *natural* desire in a Christian. It is in us from the moment we are born again!

Where do we go from here?

Before we go any further, look at these questions. They'll help you to start seeing where you are evangelistically at the moment.

1. Everyone who is born again has had some experience of being 'evangelised'. What was yours? What was good about it, and why? What was bad about it, and why?
2. When you first became a Christian, can you remember talking to unbelieving friends about Jesus? Did you have to grit your teeth to do it, or did it seem a natural thing to do? What were some of your experiences?
3. Have you ever been inspired by a book you've read about someone who led people to Christ? If so, what was it? Why not dig it out and start reading it again? (If you haven't read one, don't fret – I'll be suggesting some later.)

2
New Genes

When someone says the word 'genes' to you, what's the first thing you think of? I always start off thinking about that late 1970s advert for Brutus jeans, where they played the soundtrack of the song, 'I Put my Blue Jeans on', while various people hopped about struggling to zip up their trousers. I then chuckle to myself as I remember listening to the David Bowie song, 'Jean Genie', and thinking he was singing 'JJJJean Jeanie' with a bad stammer! Neither had anything to do with genes, and I had no idea what 'genes' were anyway.

With age comes wisdom, so I now know that genes are one of the factors that biologically make you what you are. They also go a long way to making you do some of the things you do. Genes are those little, invisible, blobby things that hang around in gangs called 'chromosomes'. They end up in 'cells' (as most gangs do!), which in turn group together to make all the bits that you see when you look in the mirror.

Family likeness

Genes also govern 'heredity' – that passing-on of parental characteristics which makes people say, 'Ooh, hasn't he got

21

his dad's nose!' or, 'Look, she gets that expression from Auntie Sue.' Isn't biology wonderful?

The point is this: we pick up physical characteristics from our parents. We also pick up spiritual characteristics from our heavenly Father. Don't get me wrong, I'm not saying I've managed to isolate an 'evangelism gene' within Christians. What I am saying is that when we become Christians, God brings to birth a new life within us – we are 'born of God'. In a way we cannot fully comprehend, God becomes our Father experientially.

Galatians 4:6 says that our heavenly Father sends the 'Spirit of his Son into our hearts', confirming to us that we have now become children of God, and bringing to us characteristics of son-ship. Commenting on this verse, Dr Martyn Lloyd-Jones says, 'The spirit we have within us is the Spirit of God's own Son. The feelings that the Son entertained, as mediator, to the Father, are therefore the feelings that should move all believers.'[1] In other words, the desires, feelings and motivations of the Spirit of God's Son come with him as he takes up residence in our lives, so that they become part of our nature too.

No illustration is perfect, and the gene illustration shouldn't be taken too far, but do you get what I'm aiming at? Because we, as Christians, have the Spirit of God's own Son in our lives, then we have, as part of our new nature, characteristics which he has too. These characteristics influence us to *be* as well as *do* certain things (a bit like genes do).

One of the most obvious of these characteristics is the desire to *love God and glorify him*. This causes us not only to worship

---

1. *The Sons of God* (Banner of Truth 1974), p. 237

him but to *be* worshippers. (Do you get it?) The desire to love God and to glorify him gets expressed in a multitude of ways, but have you ever realised that evangelism itself is just such an expression originating from the desire to glorify our God?

Turn to the book of Romans in the Bible. In chapter 1 verse 5, Paul says that ' . . . *for his name's sake* [my italics], we received grace and apostleship to call people from among all the Gentiles to the obedience that comes from faith'. Paul's desire to glorify the name of Jesus had found expression in his evangelism. It was *for the glory of Jesus* that Paul did all he could to bring about the 'obedience that comes from faith' among all the Gentiles.

> **❛ Not all Christians are embryonic Billy Grahams. Yet it is my belief that evangelism was intended to be a natural expression of love for God for *all* believers ❜**

OK, I grant you that some people are specifically called and anointed of God to be evangelists, and no, not all Christians are embryonic Billy Grahams. Yet it is my belief that evangelism was intended to be a natural expression of love for God for *all* believers, growing out of the desire to bring glory to his name, and as natural as worship. In fact, in a way, it is a form of worship.

Aspects of love

When we sing our praise and worship to God, we are expressing our love and adoration of him. However, as Andrew Lloyd Weber will tell you, there are 'Aspects of Love'.

I express adoration and love to my wife by saying 'I love you', and by giving her flowers and chocolates and other romantic gifts. But love manifests itself in other, less romantic, and sometimes more powerful ways.

Val hates washing-up bubbles left in the sink. I have learned that rinsing the sink makes her happy. Another thing that makes her happy is finding the toilet seat 'down'. I have learned to make sure that this is how she finds it. Some of the ways I express my love to Val come easily, others have grown out of my desire to bless her. The toilet seat and the sink may not be terribly romantic ways of showing love, but they bring a weight of proof to all the flowers and chocolates. If I only *told* Val I loved her, and never dealt with the sink bubbles, she would begin to wonder if I mean what I say. The *adoration* aspect of love is very important, but it is robbed of all it could be without the less romantic practical expressions.

❙ Evangelism is an expression of worship. ❚

Evangelism is an expression of worship. It may not be as 'romantic' as other expressions, but it brings a weight of credibility into our times of adoration before the throne of God: it shows him we mean what we're singing. Do you see it? Do you see that your experience of evangelism could be something wonderful instead of a cause for 'inner healing'!? When we see evangelism in the context of glorifying the name of Jesus, rather than as an unpleasant chore (or, dare I say, as just another command of Christ to be obeyed), then we begin to understand that it is not something that must be grafted onto our lives, but is in fact something that will grow

out of our relationship with Jesus if we will let it, bringing a
depth to our relationship with him which will otherwise be
missing.

Where do we go from here?

1. Do you see that the desire to glorify Jesus' name,
    through evangelism, is naturally in you already?
2. The desire to worship God is sometimes governed by
    our feelings. There are times when we only break
    through to the joy of worship by first engaging our wills
    and determining to bring *a sacrifice of praise*.

    Is it possible that one of the things that could be hin-
    dering you evangelistically is your *feelings* rather than
    lack of *gifting*? Perhaps you need to understand that
    taking a few, seemingly daunting, steps of *sacrifice*
    could open up the joy of witnessing to you too.
3. Have you started reading an inspiring book about
    people being won to Christ yet?

3

To Mobility . . . and Beyond!

Many of us, I guess, have grown used to living without the element of natural evangelism in our lives. A person who gets disabled at a young age learns to live in a way that becomes normal for them. They may even reach the stage where they cannot remember what it was like to have full mobility. You may feel that when it comes to evangelism you are looking at a part of your being that no longer functions as it once did, or maybe you can't even remember a time when it ever worked.

Whether you are a new Christian wanting to develop your relationship with Jesus, or an 'evangelistically disabled' Christian wanting to rehabilitate, the key word to remember in all this is 'grace'. Different people develop at different speeds. Be at peace about it – you'll get there if you don't give up. And remember, evangelism is not something you grit your teeth and *do*, it grows out of your relationship with Jesus.

❝ The greatest "fishermen" will be the closest followers. ❞

In Mark 1:17 Jesus says, 'Come, follow me . . . and I will make you fishers of men.' The greatest 'fishermen' will be the closest followers. At the end of the day, all that you accomplish in your life will have a direct link to how closely you are following Jesus. There is no substitute for relationship. Even a book like this, that seeks to give useful principles in how to develop evangelistically, will not make you a successful soul-winner. You must take these principles, and others, and work them out in life, through your relationship with the greatest evangelist.

Where do I begin?

I once had my leg in plaster from hip to ankle, which was quite an interesting experience. After getting over the novelty of walking like Long John Silver, I settled into developing new ways of dealing with life which didn't involve bending my knee. After the cast was removed, I found I was still behaving in the 'new' ways I had learned. The muscles in my leg had shrunk and the knee joint had seized, so it was much easier and less painful to carry on walking about like a character from a pirate film. However, the thought of staying like this was not a happy one. I knew that if I was to run and skip among the bluebells again I would have to face some hardship. It was the desire to live life to the full that helped me to go through the uncomfortable time of rehabilitation. I can now say that it was worth it.

Learning to express our love for Jesus through evangelism is a lot like learning to use a seized-up knee again. It can be an uncomfortable thing at times, yet it is the desire to live life to the full that should be our encouragement to keep going. It really will be worth it, I promise you!

Wherever you feel you're at evangelistically, you must begin by *using what movement you already have*. The main 'movement' you already have is your relationship with Jesus. The first thing to do to become more 'unbelievably friendly' is to spend time with him. In fact, take some time now. Begin to worship him. Thank him for saving you. Make this a regular thing. During your times of intimacy with Christ, your relationship will deepen, you will become more and more aware of the things that matter to him, and become more willing and able to please him. In these meetings with Christ, remember to include a 'listening' time to let Jesus speak to you. Then be ready to follow the prompting of his Spirit. Remember that the success of your rehabilitation depends on the closeness of your relationship.

❝ Joy is inextricably linked to obedience. ❞

This is the wonderful thing about Jesus' promise to us in Mark 1:17. If we will *follow*, then *he* will develop our evangelistic ability. It's not down to us entirely. Follow the prompting of the Holy Spirit and in only a short time you'll notice a change in your outlook and actions. Joy is inextricably linked to obedience. It cannot be stressed too strongly how important a healthy, close relationship with Jesus is to being 'unbelievably friendly'.

Where do we go from here?

1. Learning to use the mobility we already have is a key to developing our ability to glorify Jesus through evangelism. The basic mobility we all have is the ability to draw

near to Jesus and spend time in his presence. Think about your day and all the things you want to do. Now plan two ten-minute slots at different points during the day when you can spend uninterrupted time with Jesus.

2. From today, plan in two ten-minute sessions each day as you read through this book.

3. What 'degree of movement' do you feel you already have? When you think of evangelism, what is comfortable for you and what starts to be uncomfortable?

4. In your 'ten-minute times' with Jesus, make sure you are not doing all the talking! Give time to listening to what God is saying. Is he prompting you to do anything? If so, it probably will only involve using the 'degree of movement' you already have. (He won't be asking you to run before you can walk.) Do as he asks, and when you next meet with the friend who is going through this book with you, tell them how things went.

4
Eat Your Greens!

The next principle in learning to use what movement you already have is *diet*. Without food, people become terminally passive. Without evangelistic food, you will quickly become passive towards wanting to glorify God by leading people to Christ too, and possibly go back to disability. I find that I can be helped to stay motivated by a balanced diet of *reading*.

Now this may just be something that helps me, but I'm sure it will help you too. The accounts of men and women who have lived in such a way as to glorify God evangelistically make stirring reading. I mentioned before that the life of Jim Elliot has been a major influence on me, and I strongly recommend to you the books about him written by his wife, Elisabeth Elliot.

As you read about people like William Booth (founder of the Salvation Army), George Whitefield, John Wesley, John Newton (converted slave-trader who wrote the hymn 'Amazing Grace'), you can't help but be inspired by their example. Their lives show us what ordinary Christians were able to become by following the prompting of the Holy Spirit in their lives, and on this basis, who knows what we may become if we do the same!

In Chapter 1, I asked if you had ever been inspired by a book about someone who led people to Christ, and I suggested that you dig it out and read it again. Did you do it? If so, keep going! If you didn't, because you haven't read an inspiring one before, then turn to the 'Further recommended reading' list on page 187, where there's a list of some of the books I have read that have stoked the fire within. Why not get a couple of them and start 'munching' on these wonderful appetisers?

Prayer changes things – and people!

All this reading soon begins to have an effect (hopefully not an anaesthetic one!), the main one being that you start to notice people again, and begin to find yourself *praying* for those you know are not believers. (Notice I don't say 'unbelieving friends' because you may not have any at this point.) I started to find I was even praying for strangers. Just the other day as I walked to work I noticed a 'lollipop man' stopping the traffic to let the children cross. Something about him touched me. I didn't know who he was or what his name was, what things were happening in his life or anything about him, but I felt a strong urge to pray for him, that the knowledge of the loving God might reach him, that Jesus would save this man, that he might not be lost. I had no chance to speak to him, and I didn't make an opportunity either, but I wondered, 'Am I the only person to be lifting this man before the throne of God in prayer? Has anyone in all that man's life ever called on God on his behalf before?'

All I know is that someone has now, and somewhere along the line this can make a difference. It is a powerful thing to pray for people's salvation, because you are praying the heart of God. Today, you may be the only person ever to have lifted a particular individual to God and asked him to break into their life. It may be all you do, but it is never wasted.

> ❛ It is a powerful thing to pray for people's salvation, because you are praying the heart of God. ❜

Praying for people also has a great effect on you as a person. You are changing, and those seized-up muscles are loosening. It may seem that little is happening among unbelievers, but a lot is happening in you. You are beginning to experience (in microcosm at least) something of what Jesus feels for people. You are starting to *be* and not just *do*.

Where do we go from here?

1. Plan your two sessions of ten minutes with Jesus through today.
2. Take one of these sessions and go and stand somewhere with lots of people (e.g. your local high street). Don't worry, you're not going to preach! Spend those ten minutes just watching the people who walk by. Remember, each one you see is a person with a whole history behind them. They could be dealing with all kinds of issues in their lives. What hopes and heartaches might they be facing today? Allow the Holy Spirit to prompt you to pray quietly in your heart for particular

individuals. Let the Holy Spirit bring lost people to your attention again.

3. If you haven't started reading an 'inspiring' book yet, go and invest in one today from the list I've suggested. Then start reading it! Let the life of the person you're reading about stir you. Don't feel intimidated because they're a 'Christian celebrity' – they would be the first to say that they're no 'better' than you. You have God's Spirit within you too; you could do the same as them – and maybe you will!

5
'A Heart for the Lost'?

Is 'a heart for the lost' part of the 'mobility' you must develop before you can be unbelievably friendly? This is a thorny issue! When does your heart become 'a heart for the lost'? We all know that Jesus came 'to seek and to save what was lost', so let's see how he felt . . .

> When [Jesus] saw the crowds, he had compassion on them, because they were harassed and helpless, like sheep without a shepherd. Then he said to his disciples, 'The harvest is plentiful, but the workers are few. Ask the Lord of the harvest, therefore, to send out workers into his harvest field.' (Matthew 9:36–38)

How many times have you read those words and thought, 'If only I felt like Jesus does about people, I would run to the harvest and work for him'? The reality is, however, that you don't feel like Jesus does, and so you don't go.

This is a classic scenario. I guess multitudes of Christians feel like this. However, at the risk of being burnt at the stake, I would like to suggest that even Jesus didn't go around in a state of constant compassion for lost people! Compassion is a strange thing. It comes and goes. And I think that the fact that Matthew makes the point of particularly noting this incident shows that this was not Jesus' constant expression when with unbelievers.

> ❛ even Jesus didn't go around in a state of constant compassion for lost people ❜

Many Christians make the mistake of thinking that they have no evangelistic ability because they feel little or nothing for lost people. They also think that before they can gain any evangelistic ability they must gain 'a heart for the lost'. This thinking is simply not true. Let me explain . . .

What do you notice when you read through Matthew chapter 9 verses 1–38? Jesus heals a paralytic, and forgives him too. He then calls someone (Matthew, actually) to follow him, he heals a woman with a haemorrhage, raises a girl from the dead, heals a blind man and casts a demon out of a dumb man who then regains his speech. It is then that we read that 'Jesus *went through* all the towns and villages, *teaching* in their synagogues, *preaching* the good news of the kingdom and *healing* every kind of disease and sickness. When *he saw the crowds, he had compassion on them* . . .' (verses 35–36, my italics).

On-the-job training

It was *as Jesus went out to people*, and *after he was already involved in their lives* that compassion came. Look at the chapter again, especially verse 35. Jesus was in the habit of mixing with people, putting himself in situations where their lives might touch his. Then he acted on the prompting of the Holy Spirit. It was then that compassion came. I believe that you will wait for ever if you are waiting for a heart for the lost before you begin to go out into the harvest. The heart comes *as you go*. Don't pray for a heart for the lost – let it grow out of your activity in the harvest.

> ‘ I believe that you will wait for ever if you are waiting for a heart for the lost before you begin to go out into the harvest. ’

Just before you give in to that temptation to feel guilty again at your lack of activity, remember this: if you are using the 'movement' you have by motivating yourself through reading, which in turn leads you to begin praying for people and lifting them up to God, you're already involved in the harvest. You may feel you've only stretched out your hand in the direction of the plough, but soon, if you keep close to Jesus, you will find yourself coming back from a conversation with a lost person feeling your heart breaking for them.

There have been times (almost every time actually) when the Holy Spirit has prompted me to reach out in some particular way to a lost person, and it has been the last thing I wanted to do. I could think of a multitude of reasons why I should do something else instead. Yet, after I obey, I have found that my heart aches for that person to know Jesus. I found compassion where and when I needed it – when I let my life get touched by unbelievers.

Keeping on keeping on

All Christians are like one of the characters in the parable of the Good Samaritan. Most of us would love to be identified with the Samaritan himself – caring, non-judgemental, generous and willing to alter plans for the sake of others. The reality is that most of us are like the innkeeper – more than happy to help, as long as the injured came to him and someone else gave him the means to care for them. Isn't that like us? It's certainly how I am a lot of the time. If the lost will come to me, I'll bend over backwards to share Jesus with them, and if it looks like getting expensive, well, there's always the church resources to rely on . . .

I find I only get this way if I stay away from lost people, stop being motivated by inspirational reading and neglect my times alone with Jesus. I have also learned that the lost will never beat down my door to find out about him. The danger of a drift back to passivity is a very real one, so be on your guard. You have started well – keep it up!

One of the things that helps me when I start feeling like this is to go and stand in a busy railway station or shopping precinct. As I stand and watch people, I wonder what's going on in their lives – what joys, what tragedies? Then I wonder if, in all this crowd of people, I am the only Christian. It doesn't make me feel guilty, but it does cause me to start to pray. Then I find I have let go of my 'innkeeper' attitude and I'm back in the harvest again.

Where do we go from here?

1. Keep planning your ten-minute sessions with Jesus each day from now on. During these times, thank him that, because he had compassion for you, he came and got involved in your life. Ask him to help you develop more

'mobility' so that, as you follow his prompting, you might experience similar compassion as well.

2. Continue reading your inspiring book.

3. 'Going' and 'doing' as he felt prompted created compassion for people in Jesus' life; *seeing* the multitudes released it further. You won't *see* if you're not *looking*.

    Take one of your ten-minute sessions to go with Jesus and watch people as you did last time. Talk to him about what you see. Let him prompt you to pray again for individuals. You are 'going' by using what mobility you have, remember. By looking and praying, you will start *seeing* lost people, and compassion will be released further in your life.

4. Keep a record of how you get on in your ten-minute sessions with Jesus, both in worship and in going where the people are. Note the things the Holy Spirit says to you, and discuss them with your Christian friend when you next get together.

6

The Key to Successful Enthusiasm

We've seen that 'a heart for the lost' (as traditionally understood) is not something we have to have before we can be
evangelistically successful. But Proverbs 11:30 tells us about
something we *do* need: *wisdom* is the key to successful enthusiasm!

> ❛ Enthusiasm without wisdom is a dangerous
> thing. ❜

Enthusiasm without wisdom is a dangerous thing. I
made this dramatic discovery while working as a landscape gardener a few years ago. I had taken the works
van to the garage to fill it with petrol, and decided to
give it some oil at the same time. I had always been
impressed by those American films where the garage
attendant up-ends the oil-can into the engine while
rushing round to fill up the 'gas', and felt sure I could do
the same. All I needed was the opportunity, and now it
had arrived!

Fools rush in . . . ?

Did I first check the dipstick to see if the van needed oil? No.
Did it occur to me that garage attendants in the films never
used anything as big as a *five-litre* can of oil? No.

As I drove out of the garage, I could tell something wasn't
right. The engine seemed somewhat sluggish and jumpy. One
look in the rear-view mirror made my blood turn to ice. The
exhaust pipe of the van had turned into an industrial
chimney: the filthy cloud it belched forth engulfed the entire
landscape (or so it seemed).

I prayed.

I prayed with an intensity that had been previously
unknown to me. I drove around, desperately hoping that
some of the oil would burn off – but the cloud just pumped
out harder, stretching upwards and outwards in every direction.

Wide-eyed, I gripped the wheel and drove on. An old
man with a black Labrador, walking on the path by the
road, watched with even wider eyes as I headed towards
them. There was nowhere for them to run – even if either of
them had been able to. Both stood, calmly accepting what
was about to happen with that quiet dignity that the elderly
often possess. I thundered past, and the old man and his
dog were engulfed in the fog. My plan was obviously not
working. I eventually decided to turn round and head for
home, where I could attempt to drain the excess oil from the
engine.

Going back the way I'd come I was amazed to find the oil
smoke still hovering over the road away into the distance,
only now beginning to thin and break up. Two figures

loomed out of the cloud – the old man and his Labrador! I winced sympathetically as I 'crop dusted' them both for the second time. I couldn't make out what the old man 'mouthed' at me as I passed, but it seemed that this time I had touched another, less positive characteristic sometimes found in the elderly.

Later that afternoon, when all was well again, I reflected on the lesson I had learnt. Enthusiasm is a great thing – but wisdom makes it even greater.

A great combination

Enthusiasm to see people become Christians is a great thing, but I guess we have all met people on occasions whose enthusiasm to evangelise was spoilt by their lack of wisdom. The Bible frequently refers to the need for wisdom in such circumstances, reminding us that '. . . he who wins souls is wise' (Proverbs 11:30), and counselling us to 'be wise in the way you act towards outsiders; make the most of every opportunity' (Colossians 4:5).

You may by now be feeling a degree of enthusiasm to see unbelievers know something of the love of Jesus for them. Enthusiasm needs to be harnessed with wisdom. A horse harnessed to a cart can draw a greater load than it can carry on its back. Enthusiasm harnessed with wisdom can carry a lot more of Jesus to unbelievers, and with greater effect, than enthusiasm acting alone. Developing wisdom in our friendship with unbelievers is all part of developing greater 'mobility'.

Much of the wisdom needed to win souls is plain common sense, though there is a wisdom in bringing people to Christ that comes partly from the Holy Spirit and partly from experience. The wisdom that comes with experience you will acquire given time and opportunity, but the 'wisdom to win souls' that the Holy Spirit imparts you can begin asking for now. James 1:5 encourages us to do just that: 'If any of you lacks wisdom, he should ask God, who gives generously to all without finding fault; and it will be given to him.'

Part of the process

A vital piece of 'wisdom' is to understand that successful evangelism is a relational process that both you and the Holy Spirit are involved in. Jesus' teaching shows us that this is true.

> He also said, 'This is what the kingdom of God is like. A man scatters seed on the ground. Night and day, whether he sleeps or gets up, the seed sprouts and grows, though he does not know how. All by itself the soil produces corn – first the stalk, then the ear, then the full kernel in the ear. As soon as the grain is ripe, he puts the sickle to it, because the harvest has come.' (Mark 4:26–29)

- *'All by itself the soil produces corn'* – the Holy Spirit is the 'agent' of salvation, drawing people to faith in Christ.
- *'First the stalk, then the ear, then the full kernel in the ear'* – it's a process! Wheat grows towards maturity and needs different types of 'input' (fertiliser, sun, rain) at different stages of its development. As we develop our friendship with people, so they grow more open to what

we have to say about Jesus, and take steps closer to
him. They can handle different amounts of 'input' at
different stages in their growth towards faith. Some
'grow' quickly, others more slowly, but the growth principle is true of all.

● *'As soon as the grain is ripe, he puts the sickle to it,
because the harvest has come'* – there is a time for
reaping, but not before there is something to reap.

Many people get frustrated because they 'shared the gospel'
with a friend but their friend wasn't interested and didn't
become a Christian. They think their evangelism 'failed'.
The 'failure' was that the Christian was looking to reap at a
time when there was nothing to reap!

Time given to developing true friendship, to letting your
relationship with Jesus spill out naturally, *is* evangelism. It
is part of the process that draws people to open up more
and more to the gospel message. The more open they
become, the more of the message we can successfully share
with them. The closer they come to faith, the more obvious
it becomes – as with a ripening wheat-field. Through *relationship* you should be able to tell how far along the process
of 'stalk, ear, grain' they are, and see just when it is right to
'put the sickle in'! (We'll look at 'how' to put the sickle in
later!)

Realising that successful evangelism is both relational and
a process will save you from frustration and from feeling that
you're 'not accomplishing anything'. True friendship evangelism lives out Galatians chapter 6 verse 9: 'Let us not
become weary in doing good, for at the proper time we will
reap a harvest if we do not give up.'

Where do we go from here?

1. Keep praying for people the Holy Spirit points out to
    you as you go through your day. Pray for God's blessing
    upon them, for the Holy Spirit to work in their lives
    drawing them to Jesus, for God to show them mercy and
    save them, and for them to experience God breaking
    into whatever issues they may be having to deal with in
    life.

2. Ask God to give you 'wisdom' to win souls! Ask him for
    the wisdom that comes from the Holy Spirit and for the
    wisdom that comes through experience. Can you think
    of a 'wise' practical outworking of your enthusiasm
    today?

3. Do you understand that successful evangelism is both
    relational and a process? Thinking of the 'stalk, ear,
    grain' analogy, can you tell how far along the process to
    faith your unbelieving friends are?

4. Keep reading! If you've already finished one 'inspiring'
    book, grab another!

Now it's time to look at further ways in which we can develop
'movement and mobility' in our evangelistic 'muscles', by
examining how friendly we already are . . .

7

A Trip Around the Bay

Have you heard of 'The Dingle Dolphin'? Apparently, there's a bay in Southern Ireland called Dingle Bay, where a wild dolphin comes to swim around with folks like you and me. And folk, just like you and me, apparently, are 'wild' about swimming around with him!

People like dolphins, don't they? I'm told that dolphins are intelligent and can communicate with each other over vast distances. They are smart and cuddly (without being furry, which is a rarity). But dolphins are not wimps – they are quick on their fins and have an agility unrivalled by other *cetaceans* (technical name for whales, dolphins, porpoises and all that bunch). They also have a tooth-filled jaw that could take your leg off, though their peaceable nature means they're more likely to squeak at you . . . or is it to their friend 4,000 miles away?

Sharks, on the other hand, wouldn't feature on most people's creatures-I'd-like-to-be-in-the-water-with list. Sharks have a tooth-filled jaw that would take both your legs off at the hip, and the only message they communicate over vast distances to their mates is 'Grub's up'! Sharks are not social creatures: they look out for themselves and let the others 'look out'! Hardly surprising then that most sane people would choose to swim with a dolphin rather than a great white shark. Interaction with a dolphin is far more enjoyable – and offers more of a future!

And the point is . . .

As a person, is your character more like a shark or a dolphin? Do people find it easy to get along with you? Have you cultivated an atmosphere of friendliness about you that is not just reserved for people you know but for strangers as well? Do people like your company, or do they try to keep out of your way? This may sound stupid, but just think about it for a moment.

> **❛ As a person, is your character more like a shark or a dolphin? ❜**

People these days often walk around in their own little world, 'blanking out' other folk around them. Our parents brought us up not to 'talk to strangers', with the result that we often view all strangers with suspicion. Bad experiences of human nature only tend to reinforce this attitude, so that we build invisible walls of social protection around us. Naturally speaking, this leads to a more 'shark-like' character, causing us to be less and less sociable as a society.

To successfully communicate something of the love of God, we must get over these walls to reach the person on the other side, but we need to take steps to remove the wall around our own lives, and deal with the 'sharky-ness' in ourselves, before we can seek to dismantle it in other people. Wonderfully, you can often do both at the same time . . .

Risk it!

For a year and a half I commuted to work in London by train. At the same time each day, I left my house and headed for the station. My twenty-minute walk took me through a park. At precisely the same place in the park each day, I would pass the same man walking in the opposite direction. It happened again and again: we would pass each other without saying a word or even acknowledging the other's existence (a phenomenon well known to commuters).

I was, by this time in my Christian life, attempting to regain the use of my evangelistic ability, so it wasn't long before I began to wonder about how I could communicate something of God to this man. After much thought, I decided that as I passed him in the park the following day, I would look him in the eye and – *smile*!

The next morning my heart was racing as I entered the park; I turned the corner and there he was, striding towards me. As we passed, he looked up for a split second and in that 'make or break' moment, I used 'Evangelism Technique Number One'! My smile caught him off guard, just for a second, till he regained his composure, but I knew that at the same time as I had started to demolish the wall around myself, I had also taken a 'brick' out of the wall around him. I felt elated!

As the week progressed, I used 'ET1' every day. I found I was becoming more open with people, and this was getting to be fun. By the end of the week, I had developed 'Evangelism Technique Number Two', which involved saying, 'All right?' as well as smiling! The wonderful thing about 'ET2' is that it draws a response from a person, maybe 'Hi' or something like that – and some more of the wall comes down.

OK, I'm being funny, but I seriously found that a smile and a greeting to a stranger *changed me as a person*. The social barrier I carried around started to disappear, and I noticed that my newly developing friendliness was also breaking down barriers in those I was no longer ignoring. The 'sharky-ness' of my character was changing into 'dolphin-ness' . . . I was becoming a person that even strangers seemed to enjoy meeting.

Eternal results

The chap in the park was by now saying 'Hi' to me, sometimes before I said it to him. I was smiling and saying 'All right?' to the folk on the train too – not to all of them, but to one chap in particular. He would get on at the station after mine, sit in the seat opposite me, then take out his book and start reading. I would smile and say 'All right?', and he soon began to do the same back.

About a month later, I met him walking up our local high street one evening. We both recognised each other at the same time and said hello.

'Strange to see someone you know from the train when they're not on it!' he said. I agreed and we started to chat.

'What brings you here?' I asked. 'I thought you lived further down the line.'

'I've just moved into the area,' he explained, 'and I'm

looking around to see what there is to do in the evenings. Do you know of anything that goes on here?'

'Actually, I do, as it happens,' I replied, and proceeded to tell him about the church.

We had a guest service coming up, so I invited him to come. To my surprise, he said he would love to. I met him on the Sunday outside the station, and we walked up to the church guest service together. That evening, Ken (my new friend) heard the gospel message. I don't know how many times he had heard it before, but this time it struck home for him. At the end of the evening, he gave his life to Christ and was 'born again'.

The following day, on the train, he spent the whole journey talking about Jesus with tears of joy in his eyes. Shortly afterwards, Ken was baptised in water and the Holy Spirit and stayed in the church until his work as a chef took him to another part of the country. My own commuting days came to an end when I changed my job, and my contact with the man in the park got no further than our daily exchange of greeting.

‘ Those we are initially friendly to may not be the people we see won to Christ, but they help something to change in us. ’

Those we are initially friendly to may not be the people we see won to Christ, but they help something to change in us. They help us to become people who are better prepared to face other opportunities. If I had kept 'closed off' towards strangers, ignoring them and treating them suspiciously like many people do, I can't say that Ken would *not* have become a Christian, but I can say that I would not have been the person who had the joy of leading him to Christ. Smiling and saying hello seems silly and insignificant, but it's often the simplest things that have the greatest impact.

Happy landings

Aeroplanes need a runway to land on, and someone has to build that runway. The gospel message is like an aeroplane carrying a precious cargo of forgiveness, freedom from sin and the offer of a relationship with God. It needs a clear runway in a person's life to make a successful landing. Without that landing strip, the 'plane' *can* touch down – but it will wreck both the plane and the surrounding area.

Building a runway always starts with a workman digging the first hole with his shovel. Compared to the amount of work still needed to complete the job, that first shovel-hole looks pathetic. But it is a vital part of the work – the first step in a chain of events that will end up bringing cargo-laden planes to that area. The rest of the work must still be done (some of it harder work too), or still nothing will be able to land, but that first hole starts something that will not become a reality without it.

A smile and a greeting to a stranger seems pathetic when compared to the rest of the work needed to see that person won to Christ, but it starts something that (if the rest of the work is done too) will build a runway in their life for the gospel to land on with success.

Runway-building takes a work-force to accomplish, not just one person. So by being unbelievably friendly towards a stranger, you may only put in the first 'shovel', but others may come along and build on what you've done. I can't help wondering sometimes if in heaven I'll meet up with that man I first saw in the park; maybe right now someone is building on the seemingly insignificant thing I started?

Where do we go from here?

1. Have you found that you are beginning to be more aware of people around you recently? What have you noticed about people?
2. Ask your Christian friend if they think you are more like a shark or a dolphin. (Tell them not to lie!)
3. Are there times when you are more like a shark and other times when you're more like a dolphin? Note what some of these times are. (For example, are you more often like a shark when with unbelievers?)
4. In your ten-minute times with Jesus, ask him to help you to break down some of those social barriers we all like to hide behind.
5. During the week ahead, try using 'Evangelism Techniques One and Two'!

In our next step towards greater 'mobility', we'll look at the level of contact we already have with people who don't know Jesus.

8

Anoraks Anonymous

When you became a Christian, you didn't stop being human. By that I mean that you probably still have many of the same interests you had before – hopefully just the non-sinful ones! We all have common interests with other people that can provide points of contact for relationships to develop. Finding that someone likes the same sport or hobby as you (especially if it's unusual), tends to stimulate conversation anyway, but it also gives you common ground with them from which you can develop a friendship. It's like another piece of the 'runway' that we can build for the future.

As with 'Evangelism Techniques One and Two', you may not see all these relationships developing into 'new birth', but the point is that some of them might, which is reason enough to go for it. You can also learn some amazing lessons about how to share your faith when talking with someone about a common point of interest . . .

People love talking about things they love, and will often get 'evangelistic' about it, trying to get you more interested too. I have a neighbour who loves scuba diving. He likes it so much that he would love to get others into it as well, and often says I should give it a try. His excitement about scuba diving is infectious and makes me want to go with him. As our friendship develops, my hope and prayer is that my excitement about Jesus will prove just as infectious too.

This is the secret of successful evangelism – an excitement about the things of God that people who are not Christians can't help getting infected with. In the words of C. T. Studd, the English cricketer who became a missionary, 'Salvation is like smallpox [a contagious disease of the time]; if you've truly got it, you'll give it to others.'

Join the club?

I know people who have developed into their most evangelistic by joining a secular sports club, sharing a common interest and making friends who then become Christians. I also know people who joined a club to make friends and win them to Christ, but ended up getting nowhere. People like 'Evangelistic Fred'.

Evangelistic Fred wants to meet unbelievers and 'win them to Christ'. He knows which end of a snooker cue to hit the ball with, so he joins a snooker club to get to know the folks there. After ten weeks he's frustrated, he's getting beaten all the time, he's had a few conversations (all about snooker) and no one's so much as commented on his fish badge yet! Fred's starting to wonder if the Lord is 'shutting the door' on his snooker evangelism. Or maybe he's under attack from the devil, who's blocking Fred's attempts at sharing the gospel. Fred's not too sure.

Fred takes a break (no pun intended) from the club on the eleventh week, but goes along late on the twelfth. By the thirteenth week, he's stopped going altogether, another soldier dead in the war of 'doing' evangelism.

> **❝ If I'm in a painting class with others, I'm talking about composition rather than conversion. ❞**

There are a few interests you can pursue that you don't have to concentrate on while doing them. When I'm painting watercolours, I'm thinking about painting not predestination. If I'm in a painting class with others, I'm talking about composition rather than conversion. And when I did try scuba diving, I nearly drowned trying to talk about anything! This is where some Christians (not us, of course) can get frustrated, like Fred did.

They didn't expect people to start asking 'What must I do to be saved?' by the end of the first game of snooker on the first week, but if they're honest, they thought there might have been some conviction of sin in their acquaintances by the time they potted the yellow during the third game of the eighth week!

> **❝ Joining a club is about having a time in your week where you are assured of mixing with unbelievers *just for the fun of it!* ❞**

Common interests are the foundations for relationship. They're the starting-point you can build something or nothing on. When you're playing snooker, play snooker, talk snooker – don't try looking for 'snooker-ish' analogies for sharing the gospel (corner pocket like the empty tomb that the white stone rolled away from – or something equally sad). Joining a club is about having a time in your week where you are assured of mixing with unbelievers *just for the fun of it!*

I found that it was in the pub *after* scuba diving that I started to develop friendships with people. Yes, the J. C. we talked about was more Jacques Cousteau than Jesus Christ, but by the end of the evening Jesus was part of the conversation too.

Joining a club is a great idea – for meeting people and building the foundation of future friendship – but you may need to recognise that these foundations are more likely to get built in the pub or bar afterwards than during the activities themselves. And this will take time (and money, especially if it's your round!). You can't go running off to a prayer meeting on the same night after your club if you want to build a serious degree of friendship.

'And the next subject is . . .'

Having said all that, there *are* sports or interests you can get involved in which have what I call an 'open subject' social element to them. I have to say that I find golf incredibly boring, but one thing golf has going for it is this element of 'open subject' socialising. By that I mean that there's time for chat (about anything at all) as you walk between the holes. The 'concentration time' of hitting the ball is fairly short in the context of a whole round, and so the rest of the time is available for an open subject conversation, where you can let your enthusiasm for Jesus leak out in a relaxed way, because you're not cutting across any 'business in hand'.

Fishing is another 'open subject' sport. As long as you're

sitting near your friend, on the same side of the river bank, you can talk about life, the universe, maggots and sweetcorn and . . . Jesus.

If you have a hobby that includes 'open subject' social time in it, then you're onto a winner. If your hobby doesn't have this, don't whatever you do give it up in favour of golf. Keep doing your hobby because through it you will meet other people with that shared interest. But make sure you take time to socialise with the people you meet afterwards.

If your hobby is something you do alone, like building matchstick sailing ships, then presumably you still have to go to a model shop to buy your gear, and so you're likely to meet folk of a similar mind as you there. Developing friendships may take longer with hobbies that have no obvious social element to them, but I'm sure it's not impossible. Most sports clubs have a bar and most clubs or evening classes meet near a pub. You won't lose your salvation if you go in there, but you may develop a friendship with someone who finds salvation because you go in with them.

Where do we go from here?

1. Think about the non-spiritual interests you have in common with some unbelievers. These interests are part of the 'mobility' you already have, which God can use to help you grow more evangelistic.

2. Do you meet with unbelievers as you pursue your hobbies?

3. At what point during these times is there socialising? Do you stick around for these times?

4. What practical steps can you take to be assured of

spending some quality social time with unbelievers each week? Now do what you plan!

5. Keep up your ten-minute times with Jesus. Keep reading your inspiring book. And, if you want to, go once again to where there are lots of people and spend a few moments watching and praying for them.

9
Look How Far You've Come!

Let's recap for a moment. So far we have seen that evangelism is a natural by-product of the desire to glorify God. We all have this desire, and with it a measure of ability. By using the 'movement' we already have, we will develop greater ability. The principal movement we have is the ability to spend time with Jesus – the world's greatest evangelist. Heaven is open to us and he bids us come. By following Jesus, by spending time in his presence and by obeying the prompting of his Holy Spirit, he will make us fishers of men.

● We have gone where the people are, initially to observe and let the Holy Spirit prompt and help us to pray for them, and we are beginning to be more aware of lost people around us.
● We've started reading inspiring biographies to help motivate us to get involved in the harvest and we're already 'ploughing up the ground' as a result.
● We are attempting to become more 'open' people, losing any 'sharky' characteristics when mixing with strangers

61

and unbelievers, and seeing the value in even the small-
est expressions of friendship.
● We have seen that successful evangelism is both relational and a process: people grow towards faith.
● We have started to identify contact we already have,
through shared common interests, with unbelievers and
are making our own plans as to how to develop these.

The idea behind the questions and actions in this book is not
to draw you through a programme that by the last page sees
you giving Billy Graham a run for his money! The practical
steps are there to give you something to do as a result of what
you read in that chapter. The subjects link together to
provide a natural progression in developing our evangelistic
abilities but, as the book progresses, I'm not expecting you to
be instantly exercising *that* degree of ability before you start
the next page. It can take people years to reach some degrees
of 'success' that can take others only a few months. We all
grow at different rates, so don't feel under pressure to 'keep
up'.

> ❢ It can take people years to reach some
> degrees of "success" that can take others
> only a few months. ❜

However, do keep going! If you're finding that one particular chapter's practical suggestions are enough for your
present mobility, then stay with those until they are starting
to be more comfortable. Comfort is a dangerous thing,
however, because it's also a pleasant thing – we don't like
moving away from comfort into discomfort. But if you are to

gain your full mobility, you must keep exercising with bigger and bigger weights.

That's why it's a good idea to go through this book with another Christian whom you can 'exercise' with. You can watch out for each other and be accountable to each other over 'where you feel you're at' in your evangelistic development.

In this book I'm giving you some of the principles you need to grow, from someone who may not know just where to start in sharing your faith, into someone who knows how to lead a person to Christ. How long it takes you to get there is up to you. As long as you're moving forward, you won't be slipping back!

Where do we go from here?

1. Take some time to review how you are doing. Have you reached a point in the suggested activities where you feel over-stretched or are you OK?
2. If you're going through this book with a friend, discuss together how you're both doing. If you decide to stay with the practical activities you've been doing up to this point, make a date to review your progress in the near future, where you can (graciously) challenge each other over the 'comfort' issue.

10

'I'll Get My Coat!'

Being evangelistic means, initially, letting what you know of Jesus come out naturally when you are in the company of unbelievers. It's being *all* you are, not just showing part of who you are to people.

One of the most successful evangelists I know once told me that his secret was to 'treat unbelievers as if they're already Christians'. If you were with some Christian friends and one of them was sick, you would probably offer to pray for them. Well, why not do the same when you're with your unbelieving friends or acquaintances? Whatever way you would be with a Christian friend, be the same with an unbelieving friend. When an unbelieving friend asks you what you did over the weekend, don't skate over the fact that you went to church – tell them what you thought of it (warts 'n' all). Soon you will get used to Jesus being a subject of conversation when you're with your unbelieving friends, and they will get used to it too.

Who's in charge?

Early on, as I began to develop my evangelistic abilities, I learned that the best conversations I had about Jesus were

the ones I hadn't initiated. When I was the one who introduced the subject of Jesus into a conversation, an embarrass-
ing silence usually followed, leaving me with that 'I'll get
my coat'-type feeling. I wanted them to know *all* that I was
but, rather than letting them see this when natural opportunities came up, I'd try to engineer discussions so that
we got into talking about Christ – which normally ended in
disaster.

However, when my unbelieving friends brought up
something to do with Jesus, I was able to talk comfortably
with them about him and they were open to what I had to
say because they felt *in control of the conversation*, and
therefore were not being 'evangelised'. So I decided from
that time onwards, until I'd gained more wisdom in how
to talk naturally about Jesus, I would avoid trying to initi-
ate a conversation about him – with the result that I had
more conversations about him than ever before! When
people feel they are in control of a conversation about
Jesus, then they are much more relaxed about hearing
what you have to say. Subconsciously they are giving you
'permission to speak'. As we respond to the opportunities
people give us to speak, without trying to give more than
we've been asked for, and with our answer giving the
option of ending the conversation there, then we allow our
friends to control and drive the dialogue, keeping them
happy to hear more.

> ❛ When people feel they are in control of a con-
> versation about Jesus, then they are much
> more relaxed about hearing what you have to
> say. ❜

You may fear that if you don't bring up the subject of Jesus with your unbelieving friends, then it won't ever come up. But actually the opportunity to speak about our faith does crop up numerous times in everyday life. Your friends notice the way you act in situations, and often it's not the way *they* would act – which may well prompt them to ask, 'Why did you do that . . . when I would have done this?'

When you hear this (or variations of this), you are being given 'permission to speak'. The problem is we can get caught off guard, not ready to answer (I guess that's why Peter wrote 1 Peter 3:15!). Or sometimes we can 'bottle out', not taking up the opportunity but saying something passive and non-committal instead. How many times have you 'missed the moment' because you were embarrassed to acknowledge Jesus' involvement in your life, or you were frightened of people thinking you weird? I've lost count of the times that's happened to me.

Just the other day . . .

My car got written off by someone who drove into it while it was parked outside my house. A neighbour of mine watched me from her window examining the wreckage and said to me afterwards that she was amazed I hadn't lost my temper and started swearing. I can honestly say that when I saw the state of my car my response was to think, 'How can I get angry and demand justice from the person who did this to me, when I'm a sinner myself who deserves punishment too?' I have to say I amazed myself by thinking this, as my usual response to anything of mine that gets smashed up is to explode and turn the air a delicate shade of blue – but it's true!

However, instead of telling my neighbour how my character has changed by being a Christian and giving her some evidence that my faith is about more than what I do on a Sunday morning, I said, 'Oh, I've had such a relaxing holiday I'm totally mellow about everything at the moment!' What a winning statement!

' We have to reach a point where we are relaxed about sharing the details and the substance of our relationship with Jesus without going all religious. '

Now, I know that we often say nothing about Jesus because we don't know how to phrase it without sounding a complete weirdo, and I *wouldn't* have said to my neighbour, 'I didn't lose my temper because I'm as much a sinner as the person who smashed my car, and deserve the judgement of God on my own life.'

We have to reach a point where we are relaxed about sharing the details and the substance of our relationship with Jesus without going all religious. We reach that point by being *all* we are when with anybody. If sharing the smaller Christian details of your life is a comfortable habit, you will sound much less religious when asked a unique question like, 'Why didn't you lose your temper?' The response I bottled out of giving – 'Well, normally I would, but God's really helping me to change' – wouldn't have sounded weird in the context of our conversation. It included the truth about what God had done in me, without being 'preachy', and it would have given my neighbour the option of continuing a spiritual discussion.

Thankfully, the fact that we 'blow it' more often than not won't stop the opportunities coming our way. I find that when I *expect* to get an opportunity to share an aspect of my faith during a particular day, then I don't miss it when it comes. It's when I'm not expecting to speak about Jesus that I miss loads.

Where do we go from here?

1. When you're with your unbelieving friends, do you hold back from letting your relationship with Jesus come out? If so, why do you think this is so? What are you going to do to change this?

2. Have you ever had an 'I'll get my coat' experience, where you introduced Jesus into a non-spiritual conversation and killed it? Can you laugh about it now?

3. Can you think of a conversation you've had, where a friend brought up the subject of Jesus and you had a great discussion as a result?

4. Expect to get opportunities to speak about your faith today, but don't miss the moment if the opportunity comes more in the form of 'Why did you do that when I would have done this?' than 'What must I do to be saved?'

5. Plan your two ten-minute slots and keep seeking intimacy with 'the greatest evangelist'.

11

Out of the Blue

Before 'How to Be Unbelievably Friendly' was a book, it was a talk I gave at several places. One of those places was my friend Simon's church, and one of the things I talked about was making the most of those 'out of the blue' opportunities that crop up occasionally, like a new neighbour moving into the street, or the arrival of a new baby. 'Why not drop in a welcome or a congratulations card?' I suggested. 'It's a way of starting a friendship, at least.'

Soon afterwards, a new couple moved in next door to Simon and Kate. A few months later, a sign appeared in the window saying 'It's a boy'. They took the hint and wrote out a card saying 'Hi' and 'Congratulations' and posted it through their neighbours' door. This began a friendship that resulted in one of the couple coming to Simon and Kate's Alpha course and seeking their help on some big issues in her life.

Sometimes the most unlikely things can start a chain of events that lead to someone wanting to know more about God. It's the 'runway' analogy again! New neighbours, a wedding, a new pet, a death, a new car, a child starting school or going to secondary school, a passed driving test, a failed

71

driving test, a new baby . . . All these are things which, though they don't happen every day, all happen at some time down your street. Something as simple as a card can start a friendship which could have eternal repercussions. Becoming aware of these kinds of opportunities for building friendships will lead us to one of the most powerful ways of drawing people to Christ.

> **‘ Something as simple as a card can start a friendship which could have eternal repercussions. ’**

Acts of kindness

Have you ever asked yourself why Jesus fed the 5,000? To show everyone he was the Messiah by doing a miracle perhaps? No, it can't have been that – only fourteen people there knew a miracle was happening (Jesus, the twelve disciples and the little boy whose lunch got 'liberated').

Maybe Jesus fed the 5,000 to show the *disciples* that he was who he said he was? No, I don't think so. Jesus had been 'miraculous' on a multitude of occasions before this, showing the twelve he truly was the Son of God. I think Jesus fed the 5,000 primarily because he saw they were hungry and he was being *kind*.

> **‘ There is a power in kindness which can defeat the strongest enemy and turn the hardest heart. ’**

There is a power in kindness which can defeat the strongest enemy and turn the hardest heart. (If Solzhenitsyn never said that, he ought to have done!) The ability to be kind to people (especially those who do not like us) is a divine characteristic. It is one of the characteristics that humans have which show we are made in God's likeness. Kindness can 'reach the parts' other things don't. I'm constantly amazed how, after sometimes months of sharing the gospel with a person, an act of kindness can be the thing which makes all the difference in bringing them to Christ. Kindness is something God uses to bring people to repentance, as Romans 2:4 reminds us: 'Or do you show contempt for the riches of his kindness, tolerance and patience, not realising that *God's kindness leads you towards repentance?*'

In the 1980s I spent a couple of years on an evangelism team. We spent most of our time doing door-to-door work (not for the faint-hearted!). One day, Val and I knocked on a lady's door and chatted to her about the church and knowing God personally. She was very interested and asked us to come back and talk to her some more. During the rest of the year, we became regular visitors at her house.

She wanted to understand all that Jesus had done for her and how she could know him. We did Bible studies with her and often talked for hours over the many issues in her life but she still couldn't 'see it for herself' or come to faith in Christ. After about eight months, Val and I had tried everything we knew to help her, but *nothing* had led to her salvation.

Out of desperation one night I read her Revelation 20, emphasising the 'lake of burning sulphur' and the awful consequences of not finding your 'name written in the book of life'. 'If that doesn't get through, I don't know what else will,' I thought.

This turned out to be not one of my better ideas! All that

happened was the poor lady couldn't sleep that night! Week in week out we would talk, covering the now familiar ground around the cross, but without any real progress.

I guess we might even still be doing the same now if it hadn't been for an *ironing board.* On one of our regular visiting times, our friend answered the door in tears. It emerged that her son and his friend had been playing football, using her ironing board as a goal. A dramatic dive had broken it in half! 'I've got a pile of ironing to do, and I've no money to buy a new board!' she sobbed.

After spending some time with her trying to cheer her up, Val and I decided to go out and buy her a new ironing board. We wrapped it in some Christmas paper and stuck a bit of tinsel on before taking it round to give her, not thinking it was any big deal.

When she answered the door and we gave her the present, she was amazed. She told us that she had been given very few presents in her life and was overwhelmed that we should have done this for her. On our next visit, she told us that she wanted to become a Christian. Because we had shown we cared about something that was important to her, she said that she had finally grasped the fact that 'Jesus loved her and cared enough to die in her place'. Today, both this lady and her husband are born again and part of our church.

'Walking the talk'

Had we *not* cared about her before the ironing-board incident? I would say we cared very much. We were thinking about what life now without Jesus was like for her, and what it would be like after her death. We didn't want to see that happen to her. We cared about taking the time to explain thoroughly all that Jesus had done for her. We prayed for her almost every day. We cared a lot. But it was when we cared in a *practical* way, by doing something *she understood as caring*, that she was able to see that we cared for *more than just her practical needs*. The practical care made sense of all the theological explanation!

William Booth, the founder of the Salvation Army, knew the power of showing practical care along with proclaiming the gospel message. Unbelievers can't *see* the gospel initially, so don't always understand the love you are showing for them by sharing it. They do, however, understand an act of kindness, which can often be the thing the Holy Spirit uses to awaken them to the truth.

A man on our Alpha course loved coming to the discussion evenings where we would investigate the Christian faith, but he struggled with grasping all that the gospel meant. The breakthrough came for him when, on our 'Holy Spirit weekend' (a section of the course), he was picked to play on one of the volleyball teams during a lunch break.

He was quite a lonely man who found mixing with people a difficult thing. Playing volleyball that day made him feel accepted by other people, and *valued* as a member of the team – something he hadn't felt in a long time. As he left that evening, he told me that he now saw Jesus loved him and wanted to be with him, so that he might not be alone any more. That night he gave his life to Christ.

Before you start thinking that volleyball and ironing boards are the keys to bringing revival to Great Britain, the point is this: if a person is to become a Christian, they need to hear the gospel message and understand that 'the Son of

God . . . loves *me* and gave himself for *me*' (Galatians 2:20).

At the end of the day, the 'kindest' thing you and I can do for anyone is to share the gospel with them. Let me say that again: *The kindest thing you and I can do for anyone is to share the gospel with them.* At times though, people need to taste some 'lesser' kindness before they will be able to receive the kindest thing Jesus has done for them – the securing of their salvation.

If you're washing your car, ask your neighbour if he wants his done too. If you're mowing your lawn, then do it for the elderly lady over the road too. Once again, the whole point is that showing kindness changes you into someone who *does* less evangelism and *becomes* more evangelistic. Acts of kindness make us more people-orientated – more social, less like sharks and more like dolphins. This benefits us and our character often more than those we are being kind to.

> **❛showing kindness changes you into someone who *does* less evangelism and *becomes* more evangelistic.❜**

A constant challenge to me is the fact that unbelievers show each other acts of kindness sometimes more than we do! Shouldn't we, who have tasted of the greatest kindness and who know personally the kindest man who ever walked the earth, follow his example, and surpass the kindest deeds of lost people?

When Jesus fed the 5,000, he did so because he 'saw they were hungry'. By that act, that wasn't trying to convert anyone in and of itself, some people there saw more than how to make a meal stretch a bit further! Some of the people there began to follow Jesus from that day on. Later, some of them, as part of the early Christian church, were martyred because they loved him. And they loved him because they knew he loved them first.

Where do we go from here?

1. Have you noticed any 'out of the blue' events in your street? If something is happening, even this week, get an appropriate card and drop it in.
2. List some of the things you do (like washing the car or cutting the grass) that you could also offer to do for a neighbour or for someone you know who would appreciate the help.
3. What other practical things can you do to be a blessing to your neighbourhood? Pick a couple of these things and try them once each over the next couple of weeks. If they go well, try building in some more.
4. By now you may have some growing friendships with different people who you would love to see become Christians. If you haven't started already, begin praying for them during one of today's ten-minute sessions. Ask God to bless them and show his love for them *through you*.

12
'A Friend of Sinners'?

- A friend is someone you like spending time with.
- A friend is someone who likes spending time with you.
- A friend is someone you have a quality amount of contact with.
- A friend is someone who knows you better than others do.
- A friend is someone you know better than you know others.
- A friend is someone you are willing to trust with information about yourself that you wouldn't want everybody to know.
- A friend is someone who trusts you with information about themselves that they wouldn't want everybody to know.
- A friend is someone you care about: you care about the details of their life and would be prepared to experience a certain amount of personal 'cost' to help them if you could (though you would not think of it as cost because they're your friend).
- A friend is closer than a brother.

- An acquaintance is someone you may like spending time with.
- An acquaintance is someone who may like spending time with you.
- An acquaintance is someone you don't have a quality amount of contact with.
- An acquaintance is someone you would not trust with information about yourself that you wouldn't want everybody to know, and they would not trust you with information about themselves that they wouldn't want everybody to know either.
- An acquaintance is someone you may feel some concern for and would be willing to experience a measure of 'cost' to help if you could (though not *too* much of a cost, for they are just an acquaintance, after all).

Friends – who needs 'em?

These days it is unusual for people to have a wide circle of friends. For all the advances in labour-saving technology, we live busier and busier lives, with less and less time to develop a larger circle of friends. People tend to have no more than five or six real friends (even within their church), though they may have many more acquaintances. Of course, this isn't a static situation: friends can become acquaintances and acquaintances, friends.

Laurence Singlehurst, National Director of Youth With A Mission, adds to this the insight that because the majority of people no longer work where they live or live where they work, the few real friendships people have may not be 'local' ones. So, if your unbelieving friend from work gets saved, chances are that he won't be joining your church – and possibly not even joining one *like* yours, if there isn't one in his own neighbourhood.

For five years Val and I lived in a maisonette in a little cul-de-sac. Ideal for making friends, I thought. But our neighbours kept themselves to themselves, so that even after five years, we had only reached the stage of mild acquaintance with three of them and a 'Hello' level with the rest. Once, Val baked a cake for a new neighbour and took it round in her cake tin. Her 'plan' was to call again the following week and pick up the tin while getting to know the lady some more. The reality was that the neighbour didn't say more than two words to us from then to the day we moved – and we never got the tin back either!

However, when we moved into a little terraced house in an old Victorian street, things were very different. Within a couple of months we had formed relationships with a number of neighbours at a level deeper than those we had had at our old address. What was the secret?

The need to belong

The answer is that there was a greater sense of *community* in our new street than there was in the previous one. Community is a sense of belonging. It has relationship as a core ingredient (not always good relationships either). Community is something that is becoming more and more fragmented in our postmodern society, and yet is something people still desire. The desire to belong – to be part of something that makes a person feel wanted, needed and valued – is still evident in our culture.

❛ The desire to belong – to be part of something that makes a person feel wanted, needed and valued – is still evident in our culture. ❜

Community used to be a *life-based* thing expressed primarily in a street or work-place. Now it's *leisure-based*, and found mainly in the sports club, or special interest group and (as always) the pub. People go to certain places at certain times to 'experience community', whereas it used to happen around us.

There are areas of our cities and nation that do have a strong community feel in the streets and houses that make them up, but by and large in suburbia, where a lot of us live, streets like the one I now live in are becoming less and less common. The street you live in may be like the one where I used to live, with people who are not that interested in forming any real relationship. Even when you put into practice some of the ideas we have already looked at, like cards to a new neighbour, you may still find it accomplishes nothing to speak of. At times like these, you need to know that your 'neighbour' isn't just the person you live next to, and the person you live next to may not be someone you are ever going to have a deeper level of relationship with. If there is no sense of community where you live, you could try putting your effort into making friends in the other community expressions around you – like the school-gate community, or the railway-platform community, or (as we've already discussed) the pub, club and evening class communities.

Lessons from the past

Having said all that, however, I can't help thinking about some of the early Christian missionaries. People like John Eliot who left England in the 1630s to work among the Algonquin Indians of North America. Eliot spent fourteen years learning to speak and write their language. For years he saw no fruit for his labour, but in the autumn of 1646 he finally set out to preach to the Indians. He spoke in their language for an hour and a quarter, followed by an hour of answering their questions. The following year at a synod in Massachusetts an address was given in the Algonquin tongue, '. . . for the benefit of the numerous Indian converts'.

Eliot had, at last, seen the breakthrough he longed for after fourteen years. In 1654, Eliot set about translating the Bible for the Indian Christians, completing both Old and New Testaments by 1663. He also helped to form his converts into small 'praying groups': they prayed for the conversion of their fellow Indians and pastored each other, loving one another and loving the lost. By the early 1670s, the number of 'Praying Indians' had reached 3,600, with twenty-four Indian evangelists and Indian pastors leading many of the churches.

During those fourteen years, from when he first felt God calling him to reach out to the Indians until he saw the first converts, I wonder how often Eliot struggled and battled with frustration, disappointment and doubt. When all around him were the people he longed to reach for Christ but they were uninterested in him and he could hardly communicate with them, how did he keep going? On my wall I have a quote, attributed to Eliot, which gives some idea of what kept him faithful during the mundane, unchanging days of those first years.

> If the infallible scriptures promise that all nations will one day bow down to Christ, and if Christ is sovereign and able by His Spirit through prayer to subdue all opposition to His promised reign, then there is good hope that a person who goes as an ambassador of Christ to one of these nations will be the instrument of God to open the eyes of the blind and set up an outpost of the Kingdom of God.[1]

It took me two minutes to read part of an account of the life of William Carey which ended with the information that, by 1804, Carey had seen forty Hindus and Muslims converted to Christ and baptised. Then I read in the next sentence how all this was accomplished after he had been in India for *only* eleven years. The account had taken one sentence to tell of some of Carey's hardships: his son died, his wife lost her mind and he was close to death from illness. He saw no converts for the first seven years.

❮ He saw no converts for the first seven years. ❯

We read about famous Christians going to foreign lands, then a couple of inches down the page we read of their many converts, yet those couple of inches may span years of wrestling with disappointment, heartbreak, boredom and doubt which could, I suspect, tell us more than any-

---

1. Quoted in John Piper, *Let the Nations Be Glad* (Baker Book House 1993), p. 50.

thing else about how we may personally experience the results they saw.

Another quote on my wall is from Carey's writings, and gives a glimpse of how he lived through those days.

> When I left England, my hope of India's conversion was very strong; but amongst so many obstacles, it would die, unless upheld by God. Well, I have God; and His word is true. Though the superstitions of the heathen were a thousand times stronger than they are, and the example of the Europeans a thousand times worse; though I were deserted by all and persecuted by all, yet my faith, fixed on the sure Word, would rise above all obstructions and overcome every trial. God's cause will triumph![1]

John Eliot and William Carey left England to go to their respective Indians because of their desire to share the good news of Jesus with people who knew nothing of him. To them being 'unbelievably friendly' meant more than being 'nice' to non-Christian acquaintances. It meant hardship, loss and an immeasurably less comfortable life than the one they would have had if they'd stayed at home. They faced it and endured it because they were convinced of their calling and because they knew what true friendship could accomplish.

God's timing

We live in a very instant society. If something takes time to accomplish, we're often not sure we want to accomplish it.

---

1. Quoted in Iain Murray, *The Puritan Hope* (Banner of Truth 1971), p. 140.

We don't like to wait. We want things *now*. I wonder sometimes if William Carey and his compatriots wouldn't laugh
at how soon we give up. 'Five years? You've only just started,
mate!'

Building friendship can sometimes take years. Breaking
down the social barriers and forming a relationship with a
person doesn't happen overnight. True 'friendship evangelism' calls for people who are 'in it for the long haul'.

We used to see friendship evangelism as something that
was easier than door-knocking or open airs. It was relaxed,
unpressurised and less costly. The reality for many, however,
was that the friendship was minimal and the evangelism non-
existent. Today we are seeing that real friendship evangelism
could be the most costly thing we do. It involves endurance,
struggle, abiding in faith during even years of seemingly little
or no progress.

True friendship evangelism will break your heart, but you
will be in the company of men like Eliot and Carey. It was
the knowledge that successful evangelism is both relational
and a process that sustained these missionaries and kept
them going. Understanding this vital piece of 'wisdom' will
keep us going, even (maybe) through the kind of hardships
these men faced.

When it comes to the crunch

True friendship is confrontational. You can challenge a
friend on an issue that you wouldn't bring up with an
acquaintance. That's why *real* friendship evangelism will
reach a point where the cross is more important than the
coffee. It's part of the process! I appreciate that you need to

work towards this, but there are some important values we
need to hold as Christians *before we put the kettle on*.
Friendship, as a Christian, has a purpose other than for
its own sake. Jesus himself came to do his Father's will
(Hebrews 10:7), and he sends us, as Christians, to do the
same: 'As the Father has sent me, I am sending you' (John
20:21). He has commissioned us to 'make disciples of all
nations' (Matthew 28:19). That is why our friendships are
not for friendship's sake alone.

> **❛ *real* friendship evangelism will reach a point
> where the cross is more important than the
> coffee. ❜**

Now, this may seem as if we're getting 'heavy', but the
reality is that when it comes to being 'unbelievably friendly',
this is what sorts out the men from the boys.

It is possible to reach a point in a friendship with someone
who is not a Christian where *fear* steps in. Fear of 'ruining'
the relationship by going into the substance of the gospel
and its call on people's lives. Also, if the reality of your relationship with Jesus has not been something you have allowed
to flow out of you when in their company, then it becomes
increasingly hard to acknowledge his presence to them and
admit to being a Christian. You get stuck in a situation where
Jesus and Christianity are 'off limits' and, worst of all, you
can be the one enforcing this stance. I've known Christians
who won't let me near their unbelieving friends for fear that
the subject of Jesus may crop up and they will be put in a very
awkward position. How can we avoid finding ourselves in
this situation?

Part of the nature of friendship is a concern for your friend's welfare. As Christians, this should have the added ingredient of concern for their spiritual welfare too. In short, when with your unbelieving friend, you should be feeling some degree of 'I don't want you to go to hell'. It was this ingredient that drove many of the early missionaries to do all they did and endure all they did (and it motivates modern ones too). If you will allow this to be one of the strongest influences upon you (via all we've looked at before), then you will find your relationship with Jesus *is* something you are comfortable for your friends to see and, though the fear of changing your relationship with them by talking about what knowing Jesus means may come, you will not hold back from facing it and being a true friend to them.

The bottom line is that to be unbelievably friendly, you must reach a point where you show a person your concern for them through acts of kindness coupled with communicating that what Jesus has done for you, he wants to do for them also. You may not be there yet, but that's where we're headed!

❛ Endurance may be part of the experience, but the joy makes it worthwhile. ❜

It's not all hardship though. The joy of leading people to Christ is an experience unmatched by any other on earth. It was for the *joy* set before him of winning you and me, that Jesus endured the cross. Endurance may be part of the experience, but the joy makes it worthwhile.

Friend or acquaintance?

Jesus was the friend of sinners, not the acquaintance of sinners. He had a capacity for friendship that I don't have but I'd like to have. To get it I must first ask myself some hard questions:

- Am I a friend of Jesus or an acquaintance? A friend has a quality amount of contact, an acquaintance does not.
- Is his house familiar territory, or am I not sure of my way around?
- Do I know things about him that only a friend would know?
- Do I care about him to the extent that my actions are shaped by knowing what offends or blesses him?
- Am I prepared to experience a certain amount of personal cost for him, without seeing it as a cost because he is my friend after all?
- Is he closer to me than my wife/husband/child/closest friend?

As long as Jesus is an *acquaintance* of mine, then being unbelievably friendly will be a struggle for me. My capacity for friendliness towards all unbelievers (not just the nice ones) is linked to the quality of my friendship with him. All my friends are sinners, but they are not all unbelievers. I want to reach a point where I have at least the same number of both believing and unbelieving friends. The more that Jesus becomes my closest friend, the more this desire will become a reality for me – and the same is true for you.

Where do we go from here?

1. Think about the differences between a friend and an acquaintance. Who would you say your friends are? Are any of those you named unbelievers?

2. Did you feel inspired by the stories of John Eliot and William Carey? Or discouraged? What inspired you? What discouraged you? Are you ready to invest more of yourself in those who don't yet know Christ?

3. Do you live in a street where everyone keeps themselves to themselves and your efforts at friendship are not very successful? If so, have you given up trying?

4. Do you feel God may be prompting you to be a missionary to your street? If so, think of what ways you can begin (or continue) reaching out to make friendships with your neighbours. Plan your own strategy for the month ahead.

5. We talked in Chapter 6 about successful evangelism being both relational and a process. Is this truth helping you to keep going in your friendships, though there seems to be little progress at the moment?

6. Spend both your ten-minute sessions today alone with Jesus. Think through the questions from the last paragraph of this chapter. Are you a friend of Jesus or more of an acquaintance? If you are a friend, is he your closest friend? Ask him to meet with you, and give him *all* your life again. Then ask him to help you to be a friend of sinners as well.

SECTION TWO

Running to Win

13
What Is the Gospel?
(Part 1)

A Valentine's card and an engagement ring are both expressions of affection, but there is a great difference between them. A Valentine's card doesn't cost you much. It says 'I like you, will you be my friend?' but it doesn't risk a lot because you don't even put your name on it, and you send it via a third party. It is of limited value.

An engagement ring comes at far greater personal cost. It is not given anonymously, but face to face. It says, 'I love you and want to give you my life. Will you take it and give me yours in return?' An engagement ring carries with it an enormous risk (she might say 'No'). It is of infinite value. A Valentine's card will make you feel good, but an engagement ring will change your life!

The gospel message is like an engagement ring, and it produces the greatest results when offered as an engagement ring is offered – at personal cost, face to face, involving commitment and risk.

'Friendship evangelism' has aspects to it that are like sending a Valentine's card. The things we do as we build relationships with lost people which say 'I'd like to be your friend' and which show a level of concern and care, are of great importance, but these are generally low-risk, low-cost things. If your friend is to be saved, there must come a point where you reach for the 'engagement ring', because that is the thing which will really change their life. Most engagements are the result of friendships – they grow out of relationship.

Love finds a way

I sent my wife Valentine's cards before I offered her an engagement ring, and as our friendship grew into something more, I worked towards the day I would 'pop the question'. I enjoyed the 'wooing', but I didn't swan around wondering if anything would come of our relationship. I had *set my heart on winning her* and actively set about accomplishing my goal.

When it comes to winning people to Christ, a key to 'success' is whether you have set your heart on winning that individual. If you have, then you will not just do the friendship-building things as an end in themselves, but you will see them as part of a plan to help you to reach your goal. Does that sound rather cold and clinical? Well, it could be, without the major ingredient . . . love.

My Valentines to Val, which led on to letters and all the rest of it, were sent as part of a 'plan' to win her, *but the motivating force behind them was love*. That's what stopped those things from being cold, clinical manipulation.

As you spend time with your unbelieving friends the Valentine-type things have their place, but as friendship develops into a 'greater' concern for their salvation, then that concern will become the motivating force behind your actions, stopping them from being a cold and clinical 'system' for leading people to Christ. In the words of Paul, without love your words are a 'clanging cymbal', and they gain you 'nothing' (1 Corinthians 13:1, 3).

So, when it comes to giving someone the 'engagement ring' of the gospel, what are you actually reaching for? When I bought Val's ring I paid for gold, sapphires and diamonds, so I examined it closely to see if that's what I was actually giving her. I wanted 'the real thing', not any cheap imitations! When it comes to sharing the gospel message with your friend, you need to be sure that you are giving them the 'gold, sapphires and diamonds' of the real thing, and not presenting them with something that looks the same but isn't actually 'the power of God for salvation'.

The gospel message – what's it all about?

Obviously the gospel is more than words or talk, it is actions as well. Jesus didn't just *have* a message, he *was* the message – and we need to be like that too. But when someone asks us how they can get to know God, we've got to be sure what we're talking about.

> **Jesus didn't just *have* a message, he *was* the message – and we need to be like that too.**

The heart of the gospel message can be found tucked away in Romans chapter 4 verse 5: 'However, to the man who does not work but trusts God who justifies the wicked, his faith is credited as righteousness.' Did you spot it? 'God justifies the wicked', i.e. God acquits the guilty. But why? And how? Isn't that what we would today call a 'miscarriage of justice'? Let's start at the beginning.

There are three areas to grasp when you aim to understand the gospel.

- The human condition.
- God's response to the human condition.
- God's call to sinful humanity.

In this and the next two chapters we will look in more detail at each of these.

The human condition

For years I have used 'The Four P's' to explain the human condition. I have found more recently that I am in good company in doing so, as the same headings feature in Nicky Gumbel's excellent book *Questions of Life*, and in John Allan's *Just Looking* (both well worth getting!). The four P's of 'Partition, Power, Pollution and Penalty' are an easy way of remembering how we stand as sinners before a holy God.

1. Partition

We were created to know relationship with God. Yet naturally speaking, when a person is born today, they now have no prospect of experiencing such a relationship. Why? Because of sin. Isaiah 59:1–3 explains it through a megaphone:

Surely the arm of the Lord is not too short to save, nor his ear
too dull to hear. But your iniquities have separated you from your
God; your sins have hidden his face from you, so that he will not
hear. For your hands are stained with blood, your fingers with
guilt. Your lips have spoken lies, and your tongue mutters wicked
things.

Sin has cut us off from God; it has made a **'Partition'** between
us. But what *is* sin? It is the wrong things we do, such as lying,
cheating, stealing, gossiping, yes – but it's more than this. In
Mark's Gospel, Jesus points out that 'from within, out of
men's hearts, come evil thoughts, sexual immorality, theft,
murder, adultery, greed, malice, deceit, lewdness, envy,
slander, arrogance and folly. All these evils come from inside
and make a man "unclean"' (Mark 7:21–23).

2. Power

Our physical being is under the control of something that is
inside us, within our hearts, shaping our responses and
actions to the world around us. Jesus called this something
sin, and told us that we are slaves to it (John 8:34). It is sin
as a controlling aspect of our nature that is the force behind
our sinning. We are willing slaves, though, because sin brings
us pleasure every time. However, it never brings us lasting
joy or satisfaction – even though it promises it can. We have
a cancer that we serve as our dearest friend, feeding it, pam-
pering it, spending huge sums of money in the attempt to
satisfy it, and even though we know it is ruining our lives,
we do not want to be parted from it. Sin has us under its
'Power'.

God is holy, he cannot abide sin. It is a challenge to his

authority, and to his very nature. Sin says to a perfect, holy, pure God that he is a liar, that he does not know how best life should be lived, that his understanding is limited, that he is not qualified to comment. In short, that he cannot be the supreme ruler over the universe: sin says that God cannot be God.

As the righteous judge of the universe, God would be perfectly right to wipe sin out of existence, but that would also mean wiping out sinners with it, for sin is not just some 'growth' that needs isolating and removing; it is part of every part of us, and of what we have become. Though God would be justified if he chose to destroy us because of sin, he chooses not to because he means to save us and free us from it.

> **❛ sin is not just some "growth" that needs isolating and removing; it is part of every part of us, and of what we have become. ❜**

3. Pollution

But we're jumping ahead. There are still some things about sin we need to see. Sin has us partitioned from God and has us under its power, as we've just seen. It also spoils, damages and 'soils' our lives. Theologians from previous centuries explained this **'Pollution'** in the phrase 'total depravity'.

Now people often misunderstand this, thinking that humanity being totally depraved means that we are as rotten as we could possibly be. Yet when you look around you find people (often non-Christians) displaying the most incredible characteristics of kindness, selflessness and goodness towards others, causing you (understandably) to reject the 'total depravity' idea – or, at least, that particular understanding of it.

However, the phrase 'total depravity' does not mean that humanity is as rotten as it could possibly be. It means that there is *no part* of our being or nature that has not been touched by sin's influence or tainted by its presence. If you were to look into every part of a person's nature, you would find the 'flag' of sin announcing its arrival before you and staking its claim to the territory.

Now, sin's polluting presence may be more concentrated in some areas than in others, but the point is that there is no virgin territory left to conquer. Even the best, greatest, most honourable aspect of an individual's character, though it may look as pure as a field of fresh snow, on closer inspection will reveal the dirty footprints of sin's presence. Romans 3:12 puts it from God's perspective: 'All have turned away, they have together become worthless; there is no-one who does good, not even one.'

I guess that what we call good and what God calls good are two different things!

4. Penalty

The fourth consequence of sin's presence in our lives is perhaps the most emotive. Romans 6:23 tells us that there is a **'Penalty'** – a wage we 'earn' from sin's presence and from our participation in it. The wage we earn is death. Spiritually speaking, as sinners, we are 'dead' already, incapable of relationship with God: 'As for you, you were dead in your transgressions and sins' (Ephesians 2:1). But Romans 6:23 contains the concept that if we continue to possess sin, we continue to 'earn' death: the power, pollution and partition continue all the while sin is present.

As with any wage, there comes a 'pay day'. When we sin, we earn a wage with every act. But we don't get paid there and then. We may have to bear the consequences of some of our sin during this life, but the wage is being stored up. There will come a day when we will stand before God and account for how we have lived. Then he will give us no more and no less than we have earned. Some will have earned a lot, others a little, but everyone who has an account gets the full balance shown. Jesus spoke about hell as the place where people would be punished for their sin.

Hell is . . . a God-less place

A place is shaped by the people who live there. Your house, for example, reflects what you are like – your tastes, your standards, your lifestyle. Your neighbour's house may be very different from yours. It reflects what *they* are like – *their* tastes, *their* standards, *their* lifestyle. Hell will be shaped by those who live there.

Hell was not created for human beings. It was created as an everlasting prison for 'the devil and all his angels'. But Revelation 20:15 adds that whoever's name is 'not found written in the book of life' will go there too. Those whose names are not found are the 'unrepentant' – people who continue to justify their sin and reject the gospel. Hell is a place of suffering where each one receives the wage of his or her sin.

In hell there is no peace, for the Prince of Peace is not there. In hell there is total darkness, for God, who is light, is not there. In hell there is no joy, for fullness of joy is only in the presence of God, and he is not there. God is love, but there is no love in hell, neither is there any protection, for the Everlasting Father is not there.

Matthew 25:41 tells us of the presence of fire in hell. Whether the fire mentioned in hell is literal or not, Jesus wants us to know that there is an aspect to hell which is as terrifying and horrific as flames are to us now.

In hell, there is torment, both mental and physical; there is shame; there is regret. There is frustration and weeping; but perhaps worst of all, the one aspect of God that is present there is his wrath. John 3:36 is quite clear that 'whoever rejects the Son will not see life, for God's wrath remains on him'. The anger against sin that God has warned about through the Scriptures, the prophets and ultimately in his Son, he pours out in hell. Though hell's inhabitants may cry out to him, he is silent towards them; he said everything he had to say to them before they died. They chose to ignore him, and now God chooses to ignore them. There is no longer any offer of mercy – they rejected it when there was. His wrath remains upon them eternally – hell is eternal.

A great gulf fixed

Sin has created a huge gulf between us and God, cutting us off from his presence. We have enslaved ourselves to sin, submitting to its power and allowing its polluting influence to affect every corner of our being. We have given ourselves to the 'earning' of the 'wage' it pays, without any thought of what this means. The awful consequence of living in this way is that if we won't be separated from our sin in this life, then we won't be separated from it in the next. We will find ourselves, on the other side of the grave, *still* separated from God, *still* powerless, *still* polluted, but now with the added horror of receiving the full penalty for our sin. Our deliberate silence towards God when he was calling us has led to his eternal silence when we now call for him.

This, then, is the human condition. A bleak outlook indeed. What hope do we have? The answer is that, outside the intervention of God, we have none. But amazingly, God has chosen to intervene! He takes no 'pleasure in the death of the wicked', but his holiness and justice demand that sin must be dealt with. His love and mercy do not want 'anyone to perish', but 'everyone to come to repentance' (2 Peter 3:9) – and in the next chapter we'll go on to see how God steps in to bridge that 'great gulf' caused by our sinfulness and rebellion.

Where do we go from here?

1.   Familiarise yourself with the scriptures and concepts of this chapter. Let them soak into you and help you to truly see that however well off and secure some unbelievers' lives appear to be, all people without Christ are in desperate need.

14
What Is the Gospel?

(Part 2)

When God created human beings, we were the pinnacle of his creation, the 'apple of his eye'. He saw that what he had made was 'good' and he 'blessed' us. When we chose to turn away from God, he did not stop loving us. And his love for sinful people is not a mild thing. He is passionate about us. As Isaiah 49:15–16 puts it, 'Can a mother forget the baby at her breast and have no compassion on the child she has borne? Though she may forget, I will not forget you! See, I have engraved you on the palms of my hands . . .' Any parent who loves their child would endeavour to move heaven and earth to help them should they be in trouble, and God is the same. The difference in his case is that he doesn't just *endeavour* to move heaven and earth, he *does* move it.

God's response to the human condition

Because God's desire is that none should perish, he set in motion the most amazing search and rescue operation the universe has ever seen. Nothing less than God's personal involvement could deal with our condition.

Hence, there came a point in history when God became a man. Limiting himself in time and space, Jesus, the second person of the Trinity, still fully God, becomes fully human. And he does so in order to accomplish a work that has the power to affect every human being alive, both then and now, and those still to be born. 'For God so loved the world that he gave his one and only Son, that whoever believes in him shall not perish but have eternal life' (John 3:16). Jesus has done something that gets to the root of every person's worst problem, something that no one else could have done. Only Christ, the sinless Son of God could deal with it. That should tell you something about just how serious sin is and just how much God loves you.

> **❛ Jesus was the only person in all of history who ever chose to be born; and he chose to be born in order to die. ❜**

Jesus was the only person in all of history who ever chose to be born; and he chose to be born in order to die. Before he died, he lived a sinless life: never a wrong word, never a wrong thought, never a wrong deed. He was always godly in his speech, always godly in his thoughts, always godly in his actions. And remember, he was fully human as he lived on earth, so that '. . . we do not have a high priest who is unable to sympathise with our weaknesses, but we have one who has been tempted in every way, just as we are – yet was without sin' (Hebrews 4:15). Though Jesus was accused of many things, from drunkenness to demon possession, he never withheld from his enemies the chance to prove him a sinner. When he asked, 'Can any of you prove me guilty of sin?' (John 8:46), nobody could.

Jesus faced the same pressures in life as everyone else faced. He worked to support his family after the death of Joseph. He faced the issues of living in a country occupied by a foreign power. During his three years of public ministry, he dealt with the stresses and strains of people's constant demands upon him. All the while, he stayed faithful to all he was saying and to all he had come to do. And he did all this without sinning.

Jesus not only showed people how they were meant to live. More than that, he showed what God was like. Hebrews 1:3 describes Jesus as 'the exact representation' of God's being, and Jesus himself told his disciples that 'Anyone who has seen me has seen the Father' (John 14:9). In other words, he was saying, 'If you want to know what God would do in a given situation, then look at what I do; if you want to know what God thinks about this or that issue, then listen to what I say.'

Jesus healed the sick, fed the hungry, cared for the poor, loved the unlovely and made outcasts feel that they were of infinite value. But perhaps the greatest way in which Jesus revealed the heart of God was at the cross.

What happened at the cross?

There were three aspects to the crucifixion: physical, emotional and spiritual. All three are captured in the prophetic words of Psalm 22. Written some 1,000 years before the event, this psalm contains some amazing details about what was actually happening to Jesus on the cross.

● My God, my God, why have you forsaken me? Why are you so far from saving me, so far from the words of my groaning? (verse 1)

● All who see me mock me; they hurl insults, shaking their
  heads: 'He trusts in the Lord; let the Lord rescue him,
  since he delights in him' (verses 7–8).

● I am poured out like water, and all my bones are out of
  joint. My heart has turned to wax; it has melted away
  within me. My strength is dried up like a potsherd, and
  my tongue sticks to the roof of my mouth; you lay me
  in the dust of death . . . a band of evil men has encircled
  me, they have pierced my hands and my feet. I can count
  all my bones; people stare and gloat over me. They
  divide my garments among them and cast lots for my
  clothing (verses 14–18).

● I will declare your name to my brothers; in the congre-
  gation I will praise you . . . For he has not despised or
  disdained the suffering of the afflicted one; he has not
  hidden his face from him but has listened to his cry for
  help (verses 22, 24).

● Posterity will serve him; future generations will be told
  about the Lord. They will proclaim his righteousness to
  a people yet unborn – for he has done it (verses 30–31).

Physically, crucifixion is probably the most painful death
ever devised, designed as it is to prolong the life of the victim
while maximising the agony. Psalm 22:14–16 gives us some
idea of this gruesome and excruciating method of killing.
Sometimes we need to let the horror of the crucifixion
impact us, to try to understand something of Jesus' terrible
physical suffering.

Jesus would also have been completely *emotionally*
exhausted. The strain of all he had gone through during the
preceding twenty-four hours would have been immense. You

would expect anyone in that sort of situation to give vent to their emotions, but Jesus does not rant and rave, or lose control. He cries out from the cross, but not with a stream of expletives; instead he prays, 'Father, forgive them, for they do not know what they are doing' (Luke 23:34). He stays faithful, sinless, loving and forgiving – even to the point of death.

Spiritually, Jesus' death on the cross was the most significant event in the whole of history. This one act contains the power to change the lives of 'a people yet unborn'. In 1 Peter 2:24 we read: 'He himself bore our sins in his body on the tree, so that we might die to sins and live for righteousness; by his wounds you have been healed.' As Jesus died, he took upon himself 'the sins of the whole world' (1 John 2:2), and bore God's punishment for it – for all people, for all time. God the Father did not hold him down and force it on him – Jesus took the punishment on himself of his own free will. Somehow he took upon himself that thing called 'sin', that controlling aspect of human nature, and so God allowed 'him who had no sin to be sin for us' (2 Corinthians 5:21).

That's why Jesus cried out, 'My God, my God, why have you forsaken me?' (Matthew 27:46), echoing Psalm 22:1. The one and only time that Jesus and God his Father were separated was when Jesus was taking the world's sin on himself, and an utterly holy God could have nothing to do with sin.

Jesus' final cry from the cross – 'It is finished' (John 19:30) – was not one of defeat. It was a cry of triumph, of deep spiritual significance, because the work of salvation had been accomplished. God's purpose in sending Jesus had been fulfilled, as foretold in Psalm 22:30–31.

Going deeper

We saw in the last chapter how sin has four repercussions for us: it has *partitioned* us from God, holds us in its *power*, has *polluted* our lives, and carries with it a *penalty*. We're going to explore in more depth (and in reverse order) how Jesus dealt with all these when he died on the cross.

1. Penalty.

The 'wage' that each person has earned or will earn by committing sin was transferred to Jesus' 'account', and Jesus endured the full punishment for it: the wrath of God was poured on him for everything and anything that would never be found in the heart of God.

In the Old Testament sacrificial system of the Israelites, a lamb had to be sacrificed to 'pay the price' for a person's sin, but it had to be a lamb 'without spot or blemish'. A lamb that was imperfect in some way could not be used. The reason that we cannot pay for or remove even one of our sins is precisely because they are *our* sins. We are not spotless.

Jesus, however, *is* spotless. Because he never sinned, he was the only person able to bear, and remove, the sins of humanity. John the Baptist called him 'the Lamb of God, who takes away the sin of the world' (John 1:29). This verse shows us that not only did Jesus come to remove the penalty of our sins (actions, words, thoughts), but also to take away *sin*, the controlling influence upon our lives.

Jesus paid the penalty that by rights should be ours. It is as if we are standing in the dock, ready to receive the death sentence, when the judge says that we can go free because someone else has agreed to take the punishment we deserve.

Or it is as if a huge *debt* has been cancelled – not ignored, but paid in full. And, more than that, new *credits* have appeared on our account. The riches of an obedient, right-eous (sinless) life are found there. By receiving Christ, we are credited with his righteousness. The Saviour does not simply remove our sin and leave us empty, but fills our account with his own riches: 'For you know the grace of our Lord Jesus Christ, that though he was rich, yet for your sakes he became poor, so that you through his poverty might become rich' (2 Corinthians 8:9).

> ❛ The Saviour does not simply remove our sin and leave us empty, but fills our account with his own riches. ❜

2. Pollution.

The pollution of sin, we have seen, has got everywhere – rather like sand in your clothing after a day at the beach. Jesus' sacrifice was not just for the penalty of our sin, for the punish-ment we deserved. The Bible tells us it was to deal with our guilt as well, to 'cleanse' us from sin's polluting effect. 'How much more, then, will the blood of Christ . . . cleanse our con-sciences from acts that lead to death, so that we may serve the living God!' is how Hebrews 9:14 expresses it. For the repen-tant, the cross begins a work of cleansing that the Spirit of God continues throughout the rest of their lives: a sin-polluted character starts to be transformed into a Christ-saturated one.

> ❛ a sin-polluted character starts to be trans-formed into a Christ-saturated one. ❜

3. Power.

We have seen that, naturally speaking, we are slaves to sin.
We are not in control of it – *it* is in control of *us*. Jesus' death
was to set us free from sin's power, as Romans 6:6 explains:
'For we know that our old self was crucified with him so that
the body of sin might be rendered powerless, that we should
no longer be slaves to sin.'

A person only has power and the 'right to rule' over the
things they own. As slaves of sin, we are 'owned' by it. Think
of yourself as a house, 'owned' by sin. Along comes Jesus,
who wants this house. He buys it, and moves in. Sin is no
longer the owner, it no longer has the right to come in. It
can't legally touch a stick of furniture in it. Before, sin could
go wherever it liked in this house, and arrange the décor to
its particular taste. Now, the house is under new ownership
and sin's controlling power has been broken.

❢ As slaves of sin, we are "owned" by it. ❢

In olden times, when a person was taken prisoner after a
battle, a ransom would be set for their release. The prisoner,
carried off by a foreign power, was held captive in a land
they were never expected to live in. If the ransom was paid,
they could return to the country they were born to live in.
No longer a prisoner, they were now free to do what they
wanted to do with their life, rather than what their jailer
told them. Even so, we were made to live with God, but sin
has carried us off as prisoners into a land where we were not
meant to live. Jesus paid our ransom through his death on
the cross, freeing us from sin and bringing us back to the

place where we were meant to live . . . in God's presence and acceptance!

4. Partition.

In God's presence is where we were meant to be, but we have lived our whole lives separated – partitioned – from him. At the cross, Jesus took upon himself the cause of that separation (sin) to remove it from us. As we saw when we looked at the *spiritual* aspect of what happened on the cross, Jesus at that moment was suddenly 'forsaken' by God, separated from him. We have examined something of what separation from God (hell) will mean in the future. It was this, including the horrific 'silence' of God, that Jesus was experiencing. Jesus had known an uninterrupted, perfect relationship with the Father in heaven and throughout his thirty-three years on earth up to that point, and suddenly this was severed. No wonder 'darkness came over all the land' for three hours (Matthew 27:45), symbolising sin's presence and the Father turning his face away.

❛ Jesus had known an uninterrupted, perfect relationship with the Father in heaven and throughout his thirty-three years on earth up to that point, and suddenly this was severed. ❜

Another powerful symbol of what was happening when Jesus died is described in Matthew 27:50–51: 'And when Jesus had cried out again in a loud voice, he gave up his spirit. At that moment the curtain of the temple was torn in two from top to bottom.' This curtain in the temple had divided the Holy Place from the Holy of Holies, the most sacred area where the presence of God was. Everything about the different courts within the temple grounds, the doors and curtains, emphasised to the people that God was separate from them. Jesus' death removed the separation: the debt was paid, the offence removed, the partition taken down. The way was made open for the prodigal to return, for relationship with God to be restored.

There is another aspect, though, that it is vital that we grasp.

5. Personal.

Jesus did not just die for the 'sins of the world', i.e. humanity in general. He died for people personally.

In Old Testament times, when a person brought a lamb to the temple as a sacrifice for their sin, it was not the priest who sacrificed it, it was the person who brought it. The sinner was responsible for the sin, and therefore was the one responsible for slaughtering the lamb. It was personal. You could not come away from this sacrifice without being stained and covered with innocent blood. The knife was in *your* hands, the blood over *your* fingers.

> **❝ You are responsible for having sinned, and you therefore share in the responsibility for Jesus' death. ❞**

Similarly, you need to see that it is your sin that needs removing. It is your sin that Jesus is the sacrifice for. You are responsible for having sinned, and you therefore share in the responsibility for Jesus' death. It's personal. But you must see this also: you are the one who needs saving. You are the one Jesus came to seek out and save. 'The Son of God . . . loved *me* and gave himself for *me*' (Galatians 2:20, my italics). Jesus was willing to experience the cross because he loved you so much. This was personal too.

The cross is not the end

The message of the cross is wonderful, because 'to us who are being saved it is the power of God' (1 Corinthians 1:18). But 'if Christ has not been raised, our preaching is useless and so is your faith' (1 Corinthians 15:14). If Jesus had stayed dead, we would have no proof that forgiveness had been won for us, no assurance that Jesus can be with us now by his Spirit and no foundation for believing that we will be with God when we die. The resurrection is central to the gospel. Without the resurrection, there is no 'good news'.

Acts 2:24 tells us that it was 'impossible for death to keep its hold on him'. Jesus was raised to life because he had accomplished the task he had set out to – securing the salvation of those who would turn to God. He had defeated the power of sin and death completely, providing the way for us to be forgiven and made right with God. The resurrection was God's seal of approval on the work of Jesus on the cross: 'He has given proof of this to all men by raising him from the dead' (Acts 17:31).

And as the 'first fruits of those who have fallen asleep' (1 Corinthians 15:20), the risen Jesus is the proof to believers that we too will be raised from death. As we look at the risen Christ we are seeing what we too will one day be like, for 'we shall be like him' (1 John 3:2).

The risen Saviour of the world comes with all the riches, freedoms, benefits and joys that the salvation he has acquired for us brings with it. Here is treasure beyond our wildest dreams. But how do we take hold of it? That's what we'll look at in the next chapter.

Where do we go from here?

1. As with the last chapter, familiarise yourself with the Scripture references and concepts of this section. You don't have to know it all by heart, but a 'working knowledge' is very helpful when you have quality time to spend going through the gospel with unbelievers. Also, being able to show people, from Scripture, the particular points you are making will help them to see that what you are saying comes from the Bible. When it comes to sharing these verses with people, 'you've got to know them to show them', so get used to finding your way around the Scriptures for yourself.

15
What Is the Gospel?
(Part 3)

We've looked at 'the human condition' and at God's response to our helplessness to rescue ourselves from the power and effects of sin. Now we need to look at what we need to do, in our turn, to respond to God's offer of salvation.

God's call to sinful humanity

There was a time when the peoples of the world worshipped idols made of gold, silver or stone, because they knew little else. But now that God has clearly made himself known through Jesus, '*God commands all people everywhere to repent*' (Acts 17:30). He is telling us that we have available to us all we need to know about himself, and about how to be made right with him: how to be set free from, and forgiven for, our sin, how to be restored to relationship with our heavenly Father, how to enjoy him now during our life on earth and how to have assurance of heaven when we die. Therefore, he does not suggest, he does not invite – he *commands* us to repent.

Repentance is not a choice to be made, it is a command to

be obeyed. God did not spare his only Son, but gave him up for us – not on the off-chance that if we had nothing better to do, we might like to know him. The cost of our salvation was immense, therefore there is only one response God is looking for – repentance.

> ❛ Repentance is not a choice to be made, it is a command to be obeyed. ❜

What happens to the unrepentant?

If we do not repent, we are effectively saying that the sinless life and death of God's only Son is of no consequence to our lives. In other words, 'Jesus needn't have bothered, it makes no difference to me.'

Could a person be in a more perilous position than to be found by God holding such an opinion? Hebrews 10 verses 29 and 31 give us a pretty stark picture: 'How much more severely do you think a man deserves to be punished who has trampled the Son of God under foot, who has treated as an unholy thing the blood of the covenant that sanctified him, and who has insulted the Spirit of grace? . . . It is a dreadful thing to fall into the hands of the living God.'

The call of God to sinners lasts throughout their life on the earth. His mercy in place of judgement he holds out until their death. After death, the unrepentant have sealed their own fate.

What happens to those who repent?

To repent means to turn around, to change. It means that we regret the way in which we have been conducting ourselves to the extent that we do not want to live that way any more. Even more than that, it is to actively embrace a different lifestyle.

> **There is a difference between "ordinary" repentance and the repentance that God is looking for.**

There is a difference between 'ordinary' repentance and the repentance that God is looking for. A person can 'repent' of biting their finger-nails, for instance. They look at the unsightly, chewed ends of their fingers and determine to stop dining on their digits. A few weeks later, they are the proud owner of a fine set of new nails. Yes, they regretted the way they were behaving, they forsook their former habit and they embraced a new lifestyle – hurrah! The difference is that they found the 'power' to do it already present within themselves – their own determination.

When a person comes to God wanting to repent they are saying, 'God, I see that I'm a sinner. My lifestyle and my sinful ways have deeply offended you. I'm sorry. Please forgive me. I want to live in a way that pleases you. But unless you save me, I am lost. Unless you change me, I will not be able to live any differently.' The repentance God is looking for includes an acknowledgement that we cannot change ourselves. We 'bring nothing to the table' except our sin-enslaved lives. No 'I'll try harder from now on' – instead, the admission that we are powerless.

Sinful human beings are helpless without Christ – helpless to save themselves, helpless to live in a God-pleasing way. They need the death of Christ to free them from sin, and they need the risen life of Christ to change them and empower them to live differently. Wonderfully, when a person is born again, the Spirit of God begins to change them. The fact of their repentance starts to become obvious, as God's power changes them where they could not change themselves. Life-controlling habits or sinful characteristics are done away with; some things may change overnight, while others may be changed over years, but the power of God has been released to work through repentance.

The life-changing power of Christ is gained through repentance and faith. However, there is something special to note about the 'faith' that God is looking for.

The repentant nail-biter exercised 'faith' that they could, and would, be different. But it was faith *in their own ability*. The repentance that releases salvation involves faith also, but it is faith *in the ability of Jesus' death and resurrection to accomplish what is needed*. And this 'saving faith' is not something we naturally have. It comes as a gift from God through the power of the Holy Spirit, as he awakens us to the truth about ourselves and God, by helping us to understand the gospel. 'For it is by grace you have been saved, through faith – and this not from yourselves, it is the gift of God – not by works, so that no-one can boast' (Ephesians 2:8–9).

There is another aspect to repentance that God desires, and that is that we surrender to his lordship. This means that we allow him to be in charge of our lives. Unlike the slavery to sin that we had no choice about, making God the Lord (or boss) of our lives is a constantly voluntary thing. If we continue in it, we receive the wonderful consequences of living in the way that pleases God, like ever-increasing intimacy of relationship with him. If we choose not to allow him to be Lord of something in our lives, we deny ourselves his help and blessing in this area. We are saved, but we make little progress in the faith because we forget what we have been saved *for*.

One of the family

When a truly repentant person:

- seeks God, having seen that he loves them personally and was ready to give up his only Son to save them;
- understands that their sin has offended God and deserves judgement, but that Jesus bore their judgement on the cross;
- believes in their heart that Jesus rose from death to bring them forgiveness and eternal life;
- wants to stop living without God and start living with him;
- puts their faith in Jesus alone to save them;
- commits themselves to follow Christ until they die

then God hears and responds by coming to them, wiping clean the record of their sin. They are 'adopted' into God's family, being given the rights of 'children and heirs' (Romans 8:15–16).

Eternal life begins for that person. As Jesus says in John chapter 3, they are 'born again'. God brings them to birth spiritually and they begin a new life, united with Christ and secure in his love and protection. 'My sheep listen to my voice; I know them, and they follow me. I give them eternal life, and they shall never perish; no-one can snatch them out of my hand' (John 10:27–28). Life then centres on following Jesus and seeking to do the Father's will through the empowering presence of the Holy Spirit, knowing that '. . . neither death nor life, neither angels nor demons, neither the present nor the future, nor any powers, neither height nor depth, nor anything else in all creation, will be able to separate us from the love of God that is in Christ Jesus our Lord' (Romans 8:38–39).

You could wait an eternity and never hear better news than this!

Summary of the gospel message

The human condition

Sin has cut us off from relationship with God. We are under its power. It pollutes our lives and carries the penalty of eternal separation from God, in hell. There is nothing we can do to free ourselves from it. Unless God helps us, we are lost.

God's response to the human condition

God loves the people he has made, and has a plan to rescue them. Jesus, God's Son, steps into human history as the Saviour of the world. He lives a sinless life, then offers up that life as a perfect sacrifice for our sin. He takes our place and bears the consequences of our sin upon himself by dying on the cross. He rises from death in triumph to show that his sacrifice has achieved its purpose. He lives to bring forgiveness and eternal life to those who turn to him in repentance.

God's call to sinful humanity

God is now calling everyone to repent. His Spirit is at work in people's lives, drawing them to faith. To those who receive Jesus, he gives eternal life and the promise of his Spirit on earth, empowering their lives and keeping their salvation secure. God calls the repentant to follow in his Son's footsteps, doing the Father's will until, at death, we see him face to face and receive the reward for our obedience.

What would you do?

This book is aimed at helping you to get better at sharing your faith. I am, therefore, working on the assumption that you *have* a faith, and that that faith is in Jesus! However, my assumption may not be true! History shows us that it is possible for people even to set out for other nations, to preach the gospel, without being born again themselves. When John Wesley, one of the founders of the Methodist movement, sailed for America as a missionary to the native Indians he was not at that time born again. In his journal he later wrote: 'I went to America to convert the heathen, but who would convert me?' Thankfully, Wesley came to realise he was not what he thought he was, and became a Christian shortly after.

Perhaps, as you have been reading these chapters, you have suddenly realised that your own life is not right with God? Maybe you thought you were a Christian but now you see you are still lacking. Maybe you have been holding to religious beliefs but know nothing of a relationship with the Person those beliefs are about? Perhaps you see that, though your sin offends God and deserves his judgement, he loves you and died in your place to save you. If you are willing to seek him for the forgiveness he holds out to you, why not come to him in prayer right now?

In these last three chapters, I have only scratched the surface in terms of all the theology of the gospel message. The more you study the gospel, the more amazing it appears. There is an infinite wealth of treasure to be mined from digging into the doctrines of the good news, and time given to such study is never wasted. It will have you on your knees, humbled, full of thankfulness and worship.

Where do we go from here?

1. Re-read these last three chapters. Have you taken in all the points I made? If not, go over them until you have.
2. Copy out the Scripture references and divide them into the three sections that the gospel covers: the human condition, God's response, God's call to sinful humanity.
3. Memorise at least one scripture (more, if possible) from each of the three sections.
4. I have written a lot on what the gospel is about, but to start with, familiarise yourself with the main points of the three sections I have divided it into here. Try explaining it to your Christian friend, and let them test you on it. But beware that you don't start reciting a 'speech'.

16
The Sovereignty of God in Salvation

I remember a dull, rainy afternoon when I was about four years old. I was bored. There was still too much afternoon left before my sister got home from school and we would have tea. My mum was in the kitchen, sticking closely to the script that is issued to all parents of bored small boys. 'What about your action man, your farm animals or your colouring book?'

'They're boring,' I replied. 'I'm bored with being bored!' I whined on. At this point I would be sat in front of our black and white TV and given the choice of a badly acted 'serial' or one of those programmes where people sat around talking to each other about something you couldn't fathom. Or, if you were extremely lucky, there might be an old film on. Then, if you were exceptionally lucky, that old film would not be about a man in a silly hat and a woman with a dead fox round her neck, doing lots of kissing at railway stations. It may just be a pirate film or a war film.

I sat on the floor and waited, with bated breath, while the picture grew on the screen. My heart fell as the image became two people, one with long curly hair, kissing each other on a

pile of cushions. They looked to me like two seagulls regurgitating food into each other's mouths, because that's what
kissing looked like back then. Just as I resigned myself to
waiting for the inevitable railway station scene, things took a
turn for the better. The couple stopped feeding. The one with
the long curly hair turned out to be a man. He got up from
the cushions, grabbed a piece of jawbone that lay nearby and
started smacking people round the head with it! Suddenly
there was blood and screaming, flashing swords and death!
This was more like it! I was glued. The film progressed with
more violence and fortunately not much more kissing. Eyes
were burned out! Hair was cut off! Lions were ripped to
pieces. All my Christmases had come at once! The final scene
came all too soon.

Blind, beaten and chained, Samson stood between the
pillars that supported the Temple and began to push. The
crowds laughed and mocked . . . until a little cloud of stone
dust slowly began to rain down from the roof. Eventually the
falling dust was joined by falling masonry, people fell over
each other in their panic to escape. The roof caved in and the
walls crumbled. Then something I never expected happened.

In that moment, as Samson pushed the pillars apart,
something happened to me. All I can say is that in that
instant I suddenly *knew* God was real. I saw it. In the deepest
part of me I had no doubt.

I had heard a little about God from different people
before, but nothing of what they had said had registered
much. My parents were not believers, and talk of God didn't
happen in our home. I had been completely indifferent. I was
four after all!

But now, something had changed. I couldn't say who God

was, or where he was, or what he was doing, but from that moment on I *knew* he existed. So sudden and so real was this revelation that I actually said out loud, 'He *is* real!'

What moved me was not youthful imagination. Something more real than I can express had touched me. For the next few days I don't remember ever playing 'lion wrestling' or 'Philistine nutting', but I do recall carrying an old Bible around, telling people I believed in God. It lasted a week at most, and though the power of that first encounter faded in my life, I never forgot it.

For the next twelve years I grew into a God-hater. I argued vehemently at school against the notion of miracles or God's existence. I turned classmates away from any belief, however slight it was, and ridiculed any who went to church.

But all the time, in my heart of hearts, the certainty I'd had those years before stuck fast. However much I rationalised it, or dismissed it as the product of an over-active imagination, I couldn't get rid of it. I knew something, even though I wished I didn't know. God is real. And he was after me!

The mercy of choice

Salvation is first and last a work of God's sovereign grace. He *will* save people. He is the Saviour of the world who rescues people from every nation, tribe, clan and people group that has existed or will ever exist. He has chosen to do so. He has chosen who he is going to save, a long time ago!

> For he chose us in him before the creation of the world to be holy and blameless in his sight. In love he predestined us to be adopted as sons through Jesus Christ in accordance with his pleasure and will. (Ephesians 1:4–5)

The fact that God chooses is evident through Scripture. His choice of Israel as the nation 'for his own possession'; his choice of Jacob rather than Esau as the one to carry on the line of his blessing. However, none of his choices are based on merit; they are based on his love and are in accordance with his pleasure and will.

God has chosen to save a multitude, 'as numerous as the sand on the seashore and as the stars in the sky', from out of all history. When I say 'to save' I mean more than simply making salvation *available* to those he has chosen. He has chosen to *secure* the salvation of those he has chosen.

Sin has made us dead to relationship with God. It has cut us off completely from him. The free will that humanity had before we originally lost relationship with God has been changed by sin. We still have a free will, but now we use it to choose the path to hell. Therefore, if God did not choose to save the lives of a multitude of individuals, no one would be saved.

The basis of salvation

But if God has chosen to save some, doesn't it also mean he has chosen not to save others? That doesn't seem fair!

The truth is, if God acted fairly and justly with all people, then we would all receive what we deserve: the wage for our sin, which is separation from him for eternity in hell. That would be justice, and totally fair!

God has chosen to show mercy to a great many people, but it simply does not follow that he has been unjust to the rest. As God himself has said: ' "I will have mercy on whom I have mercy, and I will have compassion on whom I have compassion." It does not, therefore, depend on man's desire or effort, but on God's mercy . . . God has mercy on whom he wants to have mercy' (Romans 9:15–18).

God has chosen to allow some to receive justice, but to show mercy to the rest. God is the 'righteous judge of all the earth' who is 'righteous in all his ways'. On the day of judgement when we stand before him, we will see all people and all situations as he has seen them, and we will agree that he has done right. I imagine as well that, when we stand there forgiven, we will be marvelling that we ourselves should be there at all.

> **On the day of judgement when we stand before him . . . we will agree that he has done right.**

Right now you may be shocked by this. You may disagree with some of the things I have said. You are at liberty to do so, but make sure you disagree from a biblical standpoint and not from a purely emotional one. If you want to go further into the biblical doctrine of 'election', I recommend you get hold of *The Pleasures of God* by John Piper, or the *Romans* series of commentaries by D.M. Lloyd-Jones. These books are excellent at explaining, provoking and inspiring.

Simply irresistible

Because it is God's intention to save people, he sends his Holy Spirit to awaken, call and convict them through circumstances and points in their lives, until finally he draws them to faith in Christ.

'I am the bread of life. He who comes to me will never go hungry, and he who believes in me will never be thirsty. But as I told you, [the people who were complaining] you have seen me and still you do not believe. All that the Father gives me will come to me, and whoever comes to me I will never drive away. For I have come down from heaven not to do my will but to do the will of him who sent me. And this is the will of him who sent me, that I shall lose none of all that he has given me, but raise them up at the last day. For my Father's will is that everyone who looks to the Son and believes in him shall have eternal life, and I will raise him up on the last day.' (John 6:35–40)

'No-one can come to me unless the Father who sent me draws him.' (John 6:44)

'No-one can come to me unless the Father has enabled him.' (John 6:65)

Whoever comes to Jesus will not be driven away, but only those whom the Father is working in will come.

It seems that, given the choice, ten out of ten sinners would say they preferred to stay away from Christ, and that those who seek the mercy of God only do so because he moves upon them to do it.

Jesus is giving us further insight here into just how serious our lost condition is, and a fuller understanding of how much we need him, if we are to be saved. Unless he helps us to choose him, we will continue to reject him.

So God the Holy Spirit works in the lives of those upon whom he has set his heart. Through varied and sometimes unusual means (like an old film), he awakens the lost to the reality of God, drawing them by irresistible love and removing the blindness, ignorance, hostility and indifference in their hearts. He repairs their will so that they will choose God (who wouldn't when in their right mind?) and instils in them the faith to believe and be saved. He calls them personally: 'He calls his own sheep by name and leads them out' (John 10:3).

He awakens them to the reality of his existence and they begin to respond to him: 'My sheep listen to my voice; I know them, and they follow me' (John 10:27).

He gives them the faith they need to believe, repent and be saved: 'For it is by grace you have been saved, through faith – and this not from yourselves, it is the gift of God – not by works, so that no-one can boast' (Ephesians 2:8–9). As they exercise that faith and put their trust in Jesus' sacrifice to save them, he gives them eternal life and keeps them secure until they stand in heaven: 'I give them eternal life, and they shall never perish; no-one can snatch them out of my hand' (John 10:28). Salvation is first and last the work of a holy, merciful God. And the more you find out about it, the more wonderful it appears!

So where does evangelism fit in?

Salvation is a work that God calls us to take part in with him. As we go out into the world aware of the sovereignty of God, there are several things we can rely on.

● Because God has chosen to save people there is a guaranteed harvest. People will be saved.
● Because God is active in drawing people to Christ, helping them to change their minds and accept him, their salvation is not dependent on how well we explain the gospel (though we aim to be as clear as we can). This

is good news for us, because it means we don't have to lie awake at night worrying whether we said all we should have said.

- Because we don't know who God has chosen to save, we preach to *all* people. Even the most hostile or uninterested can turn out to be someone God has chosen (remember the apostle Paul). They must still hear the gospel and we must still preach it (see Romans 10:13–15). If you want to hear Jesus say, 'Well done my good and faithful servant' and receive the rewards of obedience to the 'great commission' then you must not use the doctrines of grace as an excuse not to evangelise!
- There is excitement in sharing the gospel, because we know God is applying it to people's hearts even as we speak. They may not respond then and there, but when God is at work nothing will stop him.

The controversy of theology

John Piper asks the question, 'Have there ever been any significant biblical teachings that have not been controversial?' In stating what I and many others believe about the process of salvation, I am not claiming to have it all 'sewn up'! Others would stress that there are verses of Scripture that suggest everyone has been granted free will by God to choose for themselves whether to follow Jesus or not when they hear the gospel, and that they will not naturally choose to avoid God.

In history, great Christian men and women have been on both sides of the disagreement. George Whitefield, who led thousands to Christ, believed in God's choosing to save certain people. His friend John Wesley, who also led thousands to Christ, believed all people had free will to choose for themselves. William Booth, who founded the Salvation Army, believed the same as Wesley, and *because of this* transformed our nation and saw multitudes saved. Charles Spurgeon, who lived at the same period in history, believed as Whitefield, and *because of this* grew the largest church in the nation.

Does God's word contradict itself then? Whitefield, Wesley, Booth and Spurgeon would all be horrified at the suggestion. Though they believed what they did, they were open to the fact that they did not have the full understanding of how God does all that he does. What mattered to them was not that *they* should see how God's election and people's free will fit together, but that *God* knows how they fit together. And this is what should matter to us.

❝ Doctrine changes lives and motivates hearts. ❞

The point is that we need to have an understanding of these things. Doctrine changes lives and motivates hearts. It is important to study God's word, asking the Holy Spirit to reveal its glories. Then follow Booth or Spurgeon – both ways result in passionate evangelism!

Though the Bible hints at free will, I believe it shouts out the process of salvation I have just outlined, and that's why I believe what I do. But we should never think we've got it all 'sussed' and that our particular viewpoint is the only one God should bless. God is the only one who has doctrine all sewn up!

However you believe (from your study of Scripture!) that people come to Christ, one thing you can know for sure is that they will only receive eternal life through coming to him. If you don't have some understanding of *how* they come, you will lack the wisdom to recognise at what point they are in the process and, consequently, what you should be doing to help them make progress. So that's why this is important.

Where do we go from here?

1. Read *The Pleasures of God* by John Piper. Take some time to study the theology of salvation.
2. Can you begin to see God's hand upon your unbelieving friends? Maybe they have had some experience of him already in their lives? Ask them. Let this encourage you as you pray for them and speak with them about Jesus.
3. Knowing something of the process of salvation is excellent, but how can we use this to lead people to Christ? Read on!

17
Leading Someone to Christ

At four years old, I knew that God existed. At fifteen, I denied it (though I still knew it was true). At sixteen, after some investigation, many conversations and a growing sense of conviction accompanied by the awareness of God's presence, I wanted to become a Christian. But I didn't know how. Thankfully, a Christian friend of mine *did* know, and was in the right place at the right time to tell me. He walked home with me late one night after we had been to see a band at his church. I explained that I wanted what I saw he had, but I didn't know how to get it. He simply and slowly took me through four points to help me understand whether I was truly ready to become a Christian, and if so, how to become one. Since then, I have used the same points when helping other people to become Christians. They are (literally!) as easy to remember as A, B, C and D.

A = Admit

First of all, a person has to see and admit that they are a sinner – that their lies, disobedience, jealousy, hatred, lust, dishonesty, lack of self-control (or whatever) has hurt their own and other people's lives, but most of all has offended a holy God. They need to see that their sin has severed them from relationship with God and will keep them that way for eternity unless they get help. They need to be sorry for their sin – but more than that, they need to be *repentant* (willing to turn away from it and embrace a different lifestyle).

B = Believe

Secondly, a person needs to believe that, in spite of their sin, God loves them. He loved them so much that he sent his Son, Jesus, to live a sinless life on earth and to die on a cross, bearing that person's sin. Jesus took their punishment so that they could go free. They need to see the personal element to it – that Jesus loved *them* and gave himself for *them* personally. They also need to believe that Jesus rose from death and is alive today to bring them God's forgiveness and eternal life.

C = Consider

Thirdly, a person needs to consider the cost of following Jesus. Salvation is a free gift, but Jesus asks us to allow him to be the boss (or Lord) of our lives from then on. This means that a person must be willing to let Jesus have the final say in all the areas of their life – how they conduct their relationships, their work life, their private life, their finances, their children, etc. Jesus asks this because he knows that if we live according to his instruction we can live fulfilled lives in all these areas and more. However, living life Jesus' way is not without hardship or even suffering at times, so a person needs to be aware of this before they make their commitment. Better that they take time to count the cost, then when they are ready, they will be in a better position to receive God's grace when things get tough.

D = Do

Admitting, believing and considering are followed by *doing* something. There are three things to do.

1. Ask them to pray, admitting their sin to God, asking for his forgiveness and repenting of sin (even specific sins if appropriate).
2. Encourage them to tell God that they believe all that we mentioned above about Jesus – his death and resurrection for them.
3. They need to commit their life to him, telling him that they will follow him from that moment on until the day they die. As part of this, encourage them to be baptised in water, in obedience to Jesus and as a demonstration that they have stopped living for themselves and are now following him.

New Christians are like new babies – they need care and looking after. By being part of a good local church and meeting together regularly with other Christians, they will get the support, encouragement and help they need. Make sure that if they are not coming to your own church, they are in touch with a church that will help them to grow in their new relationship with Jesus. After praying with them, encourage them to tell someone what has happened to them. (You may not be able to hold them back!) New believers should be encouraged that sharing their faith is normal and natural from the word go.

(Incidentally, by the time my Christian friend had gone through the A, B, C, D points with me, we had reached my house. It was late, so he didn't come in. He didn't have to, as I knew now what I needed to do. Alone in my room, I prayed and did business with God. After I'd prayed, I felt a great sense of relief. I *knew* that my life was right with God. I have known him ever since. And knowing him is wonderful!)

Sensitivity needed!

When we are with someone who is ready to become a Christian, we are rather like midwives in a delivery suite. We are there to watch that everything is going smoothly. A good midwife doesn't keep leaping in to instruct and dictate. She gives the minimum of direction while knowing that nature will take its course. If there is something that needs her attention, she will give it, then move back to allow things to progress naturally. She isn't constantly coaching her patient on all the technical details of what is happening, but she is running through them in her mind as a check that everything is going nicely.

Before you pray with someone to be born again, make sure they are *ready to be born* by going through the A, B, C, D with them. If they find they have a sticking-point with one or more of these, then don't pray with them to be saved because they're not ready yet. In time they may be, but first they need to work through the issues that concern them. Pray with them, asking the Holy Spirit to bring them further understanding.

Sometimes people are awakened to the reality of God but are not yet ready to give him their lives. They may think Jesus is wonderful but do not believe they are sinners, or that Jesus is the only way to God. Sometimes they are moved to tears at the thought of Jesus' death, or their own past, but are not yet willing to forsake sin or see that his death was for them. Never be swayed by tears into praying for salvation, without first clarifying that person is ready to give their life completely to Christ. Knowing the A, B, C, D points will help you not to make the mistake of thinking someone is further on than they actually are. But don't forget, this 'framework' is primarily to help *them*, not you!

When it comes to praying, it is helpful to ask another Christian to pray with you, so that there are two Christians praying for one unbeliever. You can help each other should you forget something in the excitement of the moment! Also, while one of you is going through the A, B, C, D points with the unbelieving friend, the other Christian can be asking God if there is anything you need to specifically cover when you pray (e.g. renouncing past involvement in something like spiritualism).

❛ They may not use "the right words", but is what they're saying expressing the right heart? ❜

When you start to pray with your unbelieving friend for salvation, get them to pray out loud all that is on their heart. They may not use 'the right words', but is what they're saying expressing the right heart? It's important they pray out loud so that you can be sure they are expressing what they need to say, and that they are exercising faith and trust in Jesus. You may need to help them, remind them or prompt them, if they haven't covered something important, but do this with gentleness and without breaking them out of that atmosphere of meeting with God.

Finally, get them to thank God for all he has done for them. Thanksgiving is an expression of faith, and faith releases the power of God. People are often filled with the Holy Spirit through this as well.

> **❛ They need not feel as though they could leap tall buildings in a single bound, but there should be a sense of having met with God. ❜**

Ask them how they feel. They need not feel as though they could leap tall buildings in a single bound, but there should be a sense of having met with God. Arrange to see them again that week to pray some more and encourage them. They need support and care now, as a newborn 'babe in Christ'. If you personally can't look out for them, make sure that someone will.

'We're in this together'

By explaining the points of the gospel and praying for your friend to receive the understanding and faith they need to be saved, you are doing all you can do. You must leave the rest up to God, who delights in saving people.

Salvation is a work of God in which he wants us to be involved, *not* something that's down to us that we hope he's involved in! It is a fantastic partnership. It's a bit like the dad who lets his child hold the steering-wheel of his boat, telling him when, and how far, to turn. Who is doing the driving? They both are!

The partnership isn't an equal one. It doesn't have to be for the boat to reach its destination. But this is how the dad has chosen to do it, because this way brings him more joy and pleasure. He delights in the look on his child's face, expressing the wonder of being given the privilege of steering the boat. 'I'm driving, Daddy!' says the excited child. 'Yes, you are, you really are!' says the father, as he watches over all that the child is doing.

As you seek to lead people to Christ, God is watching over all that you do. He directs, encourages, corrects and prompts your movements. Then, in that moment of joy after you've prayed with someone to become a Christian, you and the Father can rejoice together.

Where do we go from here?

1. Familiarise yourself with the A, B, C, D points so that, when you are in the situation of helping someone to respond to God, you are prepared for what to do.

2. Thinking of the A, B, C, D points can you tell what stage your friends are at in coming to faith in Christ? Again, let this encourage your praying and help to highlight issues for discussion with them.

3. Do you think any of your unbelieving friends are close to salvation? Why not ask them what's stopping them from becoming a Christian, and be ready to pray with them!

18
Can You Hear Me?

Research has shown that 80 per cent of what we communicate has got nothing to do with what we actually say, but is all to do with the way we behave. A further 15 per cent of what we communicate is in *how* we say what we do. Only 5 per cent of what we communicate relates to the actual words that come out of our mouth. So, communication of the gospel is an area that requires 'wisdom'. Fortunately for us, the apostle Paul has got it covered!

> Devote yourselves to prayer, being watchful and thankful. And pray for us, too, that God may open a door for our message, so that we may proclaim the mystery of Christ, for which I am in chains. Pray that I may proclaim it clearly, as I should. Be wise in the way you act towards outsiders; make the most of every opportunity. Let your conversation be always full of grace, seasoned with salt, so that you may know how to answer everyone. (Colossians 4:2–6)

First things first

These few verses give us a wealth of instruction about how we can effectively communicate the truths of the gospel to *everyone.* Paul begins by focusing our attention on Christ by saying, 'Devote yourselves to prayer . . .'

To be devoted to something means to give yourself to it. It occupies a place in your life that is reserved for the things that really matter to you. People often devote themselves to all kinds of things that give very little in return. In this case, though, by devoting ourselves to prayer, we can unlock a tidal wave of God's blessing upon unbelievers and upon ourselves. No wonder the devil doesn't want Christians to pray, and tries to put up any obstacle he can to keep us from it.

When we devote ourselves to prayer we are saying a number of things. We acknowledge that we are not in charge of people's salvation, God is. We are telling God that, without his help, our best efforts at winning people will amount to nothing. We acknowledge that the gospel message does not belong to us; it belongs to God, and 'we speak as men approved by God to be entrusted with the gospel' (1 Thessalonians 2:4).

God doesn't approve just anybody to be entrusted with his gospel. Those he approves are those who have personally acknowledged the truth of the gospel and who have submitted themselves to the claims it makes over their lives. It is an immense privilege to be entrusted with the gospel. Like a son who is lent his father's brand new car, we are responsible for treating properly what has been entrusted. So, as we devote ourselves to prayer, we are also accepting the responsibility to handle the gospel message with integrity.

Devotion to prayer keeps us aware of our position in the equation, of God's supremacy, our dependence and the awesome privilege of having our hands on the most powerful, life-changing message in the universe. The place of prayer is often where the most progress is made in seeing people affected by the gospel, and where breakthrough is first received. History shows that it is prayer that always precedes revival and prayer that always accompanies revival.

> **' Before you can be effective at speaking to people about God, you've got to be used to speaking to God about people. '**

Before you can be effective at speaking to people about God, you've got to be used to speaking to God about people. Paul had seen this on numerous occasions, and that's why he begins by saying that we must be devoted to prayer.

Watch out!

Paul goes on to say that we must 'be watchful and thankful'. Those who *expect* to have opportunity to share their faith get more opportunities than those who don't. This doesn't mean that the unexpectant get fewer opportunities; it means that the expectant see the opportunities coming long before the unexpectant do and, therefore, miss fewer of them. So, be watchful! Sometimes, by keeping your eyes open, you come across the most amazing opportunities.

I was driving to work one morning when I noticed a tramp standing at the gates of a local Baptist church. He appeared to be washing his hands, yet he had no water. As I drove past, he got on his knees and bowed his face to the floor. Watching in the rear-view mirror, I saw him get to his feet and 'wash' his face and hands again. I realised that he was a Muslim.

I stopped the car, got out and walked back to where the

man was still on his knees. I waited until he had finished then said to him, 'I noticed you as I was just driving past and I hope you don't mind me asking, but were you praying?'

'Yes, it was time for my prayers,' he replied.

'I like to pray too,' I said, and we began to talk all about prayer, who he prayed to, who I prayed to, whether our prayers were answered or not, what sort of things we pray about, who Allah is, who Jesus is. At the end of our conversation, I asked him if he had ever heard before who Jesus was and what he had done. He said that our conversation was the first time he had heard about it. We prayed together and I asked Jesus to come and reveal himself to him. Then I went off to work.

I prayed that I might see Shazan (that's what he told me his name was) again sometime and kept looking out for him. Two days later, I spotted him walking along the high street in the early morning. During the previous two days I had been praying for him and now I asked the Holy Spirit what I should do. I guessed Shazan was probably hungry (he'd eaten all my sandwiches at our first meeting), but not being as 'saintly' that morning, I wasn't keen on losing my lunch again!

Then I felt the Holy Spirit say to me, 'Go and buy two of those currant loaves you're always scoffing whenever you get the chance. Sit down with Shazan, give him one of the loaves, you eat the other, and tell him about the bread of life!' So that's what I did. We sat on the pavement outside the baker's and talked about Jesus. Shazan started to cry as we talked and to thank me. Again, he said he had heard nothing like this before. We prayed and asked the Holy Spirit to come to us, and bring more of the reality of Jesus to us.

Did Shazan give his life to Christ? No. He wasn't at that point yet. But he had begun to understand that Jesus was real. He knew that the kingdom of God had come close to him. I left for work again, praying that God would save him.

I never saw Shazan again. I don't know what lasting impression our conversations had upon him, but I know that he has had a lasting impression on me, because I still pray for him and it's been ten years since I first saw him standing outside the Baptist church.

Keeping our eyes open for opportunities to talk with people about Jesus is one of the fundamental requirements for anyone who wants to win people for Christ. The opportunities are numerous for those who look out for them. And when you see one and act on it, 'watchfulness' produces its companion, 'thankfulness'.

Gratitude for the opportunities that God directs across our path is a natural thing if we are watchful, ever-ready people. Even if you miss the opportunity, or don't make the most of it, the fact that you recognised it is cause for celebration! Thank God that he brings these opportunities to you. *He* believes in your ability to witness for him even if you're a bit dubious.

Open doors

Remember, you're not alone in God's harvest. Right now, there are millions of Christians going about their daily business while also seeking to affect and change people's lives through sharing the gospel of God. Pray for them. No doubt they are praying for you! What should you pray? Pray for what you'd want *them* to pray for *you*. Pray for the same

things that Paul asked the Colossians to pray for. Pray that
Jesus will help them to be watchful and thankful and that
God would 'open a door for our message'.

A locksmith can open a lock better than a bricklayer. No
disrespect intended to bricklayers, but most of those I've
ever known, when faced with a locked door that they needed
to open, resorted to a boot rather than something a bit more
delicate. The locksmith does it best because he knows the
intricate workings of the lock. The bricklayer can open the
door, but the lock, door-frame and door will probably all be
damaged in the process!

> **❬ A locksmith can open a lock better than a
> bricklayer. ❭**

We often think we know what's needed to open a person
up to the gospel. Sometimes the reality is that we resort to
measures akin to a bricklayer's boot. Our attempts at
getting past a person's defences may be 'successful', but
they cause a whole lot of damage in the process. The Holy
Spirit, however, knows the intricate workings of the human
heart. He should do, after all, because he helped make it.
He knows how to open up a door in a person's life for the
message of God's forgiveness, and though this may be a delicate, slow process, he is an expert at it and is thorough in
his work.

When Paul asks for prayer that God would 'open a door
for our message', he is again acknowledging our dependence
upon God to achieve the best results. He is saying, 'I could
force my way in but you, Lord, know how to open every
rebellious heart. I could apply the gospel like a crow-bar, but

you know how to apply it as a key. I'll speak as you've told me to, but please take those words and do what only you can do – open the hearts of the unbelieving.'

It is the Holy Spirit who opens the door for the gospel into the life of every sinner who repents. And if they are going to repent of their sin, you need to involve the expert. So, pray that *God* may open a door for your message in the lives of those you are speaking to, because if it is God who opens it, then there is no one stronger who can close it.

Making it clear

Paul's objective in preaching the gospel was to 'proclaim it clearly, as I should'. There are various aspects to this which we need to consider.

Every person is an individual. The issues that matter to one may be of no concern to another. When it comes to proclaiming the gospel clearly, you need to find the best way to put it across to the particular person you have just found an opportunity to speak to. Of course, the *facts* of the gospel are unchanging. But the starting-point and the 'angle of approach' will differ with every new opportunity that arises. In each case, you have to learn to 'scratch where that person is itching'.

One danger with failing to do this is that sharing the gospel can become rather like regurgitating an 'off-pat' monologue! If you've ever been on a guided tour to some historic place, you can tell before the guide has finished their first sentence that you're being given a well-rehearsed and oft-repeated spiel. What you're being told may well be true, but it has little or no life in it.

Now put yourself in the shoes of the person you're speaking to. They don't want to hear a recital, starting from the Fall right through to God's call to repentance! Unfortunately, some Christians are not interested in what unbelievers think about the gospel – they just believe that they need to hear it through and make a decision. As a result, there is no life in what they say: they are 'informers' rather than 'reformers'.

> ❛ put yourself in the shoes of the person you're speaking to. They don't want to hear a recital ❜

However, if you actually *listen* to what someone is saying – their objections, doubts and confusion – you can talk to them about the points of the gospel that are relevant to their particular situation. (Watch out, though, for any 'red herrings' they may throw in to divert you from talking about things which are drawing them towards the cross! Sometimes the gospel gets too close for comfort and people try to avoid seeing what it is saying. If this starts to happen, be ready to wisely bring your discussion back to talking about Jesus.)

Proclaiming the gospel *clearly* also means not talking in religious language. Most of us grow to understand the detail of the gospel message through studying it *after* we become Christians. Of necessity, the study of theological issues involves understanding concepts that are referred to by long, rather complex words such as atonement, predestination, redemption and propitiation. If we are not careful, because *we* learned the concepts of the gospel by using such words, we try to explain them to unbelievers by using the same language. It's disastrous! We've got to speak in everyday language. If we want to make things clear for our hearers, we must use the words they would use.

Any theologians reading this may be having a heart attack now, because they know that if you substitute a less complex word for a more complex one, you lose a whole heap of the full meaning conveyed by the 'correct' term. 'Paying the price' may not carry the full meaning of 'atonement', but at the end of the day, Fred Bloggs knows what you're on about if you talk about 'payment'. Once Fred gets saved, the theologians can help him get straight on the full glory of what's happened to him. (And let's face it, the theologians are only going to get to meet Fred once he's saved anyway!)

❛ I was asked by a lady in the street if I had "found Jesus". I asked her how long he had been missing ❜

Evangelical jargon is another thing we need to avoid. Some Christians' conversation is full of 'the blood of the Lamb' and other such phrases. They talk about church services where 'God moved'. (Where did he go?) I was at a meeting once where everybody was encouraged to 'jubilate' – I contented myself with jigging around from one leg to the other, hoping that I was getting near to what was expected. On another occasion, before I became a Christian, I was asked by a lady in the street if I had 'found Jesus'. I asked her how long he had been missing, and said that I was sure if she went back to where she last saw him he couldn't have gone too far.

I rest my case. To help people understand our message, we need to talk their language.

Opportunity knocks

Paul's next piece of advice is that we should be 'wise in the way you act towards outsiders; make the most of every opportunity'.

To make the most of every opportunity doesn't mean you milk it for all you can. It means you take each opportunity as far as it is wise to take it at that time. On some occasions, the wisest thing may be to say just a little about Jesus and see if that creates a positive response. At other times, you may feel it is right to press home some aspect of the gospel that is relevant to the person you've been talking to. How will you know? The answer is to keep yourself tuned into the prompting of the Holy Spirit. If you sense him telling you to shut up, then shut up. If you sense him telling you to carry on, then carry on.

I used to try and offload the whole gospel message every time I got into a conversation about Christ. I told them questions that I thought they should be asking, and then proceeded to answer those questions for them. I brought up things that hadn't even entered their heads, taking them on a journey from the Garden of Eden through to Judgement Day via the Garden of Gethsemane and the Garden Tomb. Not surprisingly, people felt overwhelmed! Not only did they not want to hear any more when they next saw me, but I didn't have anything more to tell them.

Over the years I have learned that the wisest way of making the most of an opportunity is to say just enough to make people hungry for more. That way, the next time we met, I could be sure the subject of Jesus would enter the conversation again. And even if *I* didn't see some of the people I'd witnessed to again, the fact that they were open to hear more of the gospel would make things a lot better for the next Christian they met!

However, this isn't always easy – not because I like blasting unbelievers with the gospel, but because the gospel is naturally offensive. It tells us we are not good people, when we think we are. It tells us we deserve punishment from God, when we think *he's* got a lot to answer for. It tells us we are helpless to rescue ourselves from sin and its consequences, when we think there isn't any obstacle we cannot overcome. Worst of all, the gospel tells us that we have to submit our lives to someone who died in our place to rescue us without our asking him to, and that if we don't, we will stay separated from God for eternity in hell.

People are going to get offended when they begin to understand what we are actually saying. We have to face it – not everybody is going to like us. In fact, a lot of people are going to hate us. Jesus warned us that this would be the case: 'If the world hates you, keep in mind that it hated me first. If you belonged to the world, it would love you as its own. As it is, you do not belong to the world, but I have chosen you out of the world. That is why the world hates you' (John 17: 18–19).

My point is that in the way we share the gospel we shouldn't *add* to the offence by our attitude towards people, by the way we behave towards them and by the way we speak.

Our speech is something that Paul has some wise instruction for too: 'Let your conversation be always full of grace.' Grace listens to what someone has to say. It doesn't rubbish their opinion, even if we consider that opinion completely weird. Grace brings lightness and laughter to a conversation and dissolves hostility. Grace doesn't argue, it speaks the truth in love.

> **❝ Sometimes you have to let the initial hostility in a person's attitude pass unchallenged until they can begin to talk freely *with* you rather than *at* you. ❞**

In his first letter, the apostle Peter tells us to 'Always be prepared to give an answer to everyone who asks you to give the reason for the hope that you have. But do this with gentleness and respect' (1 Peter 3:15–16). Grace involves gentleness and respect. Sometimes you have to let the initial hostility in a person's attitude pass unchallenged until they can begin to talk freely *with* you rather than *at* you. If I've learned anything over the time I've been talking to people about Jesus, it's that I'll never get someone to change their mind by arguing with them. Arguments only entrench people in their position: even when they may know they are wrong, they don't want to admit it, because they would 'lose' the argument, and no one likes to lose.

Grace means also that you don't correct a person on every detail of what's wrong with their beliefs as they are expressing them. I've seen people do that. They point out the minutest inconsistencies in what an unbeliever is saying, until the poor person doesn't want to say anything else in case they are made to look even more stupid.

People who are not Christians can be incredibly shrewd. They see through a lot of what we say and a lot of what we do if it is not genuine. If they see that *you* are no longer open to be proved wrong on some of the things you believe, then *they* will not want to be open for you to prove some of their beliefs wrong. Grace says to an unbeliever that you don't have all the answers, and are still open to find more.

Grace does, however, say that the answers you have found concerning how to know God are the *right* ones. Grace is not a wimpy thing that turns you into something for people to wipe their feet on. Grace helps us to stand up for what is true and right but to do it in a way which attracts people rather than repels them.

Add seasoning

Our conversation as Christians should also be 'seasoned with salt'. When you add salt to food, you sharpen its flavour. Having talked about being gracious, it is not a contradiction to add that our gracious conversation must have some 'bite' to it.

Be ready to question people (graciously, of course!) when they are telling you their beliefs. Ask them: 'What do you mean when you say that? What do you honestly believe about what you just said?' Bring in those relevant points of the gospel and help people to examine and challenge their own philosophies. You don't have to be an expert on every post-modern religious belief or cult doctrine to spot what the holes are. If you know what the gospel is, you'll spot a forgery a mile off.

I remember sitting in a pub, talking with a chap who has since become one of my greatest friends. At the time he was a nineteenth-level Freemason. I knew very little about freemasonry whereas Geoff was obviously an expert on the subject. However, as Geoff told me more about what he was trying to achieve through freemasonry, the holes in his belief became increasingly obvious. I was able to speak to him on the basis of what he had told me and show him how his aims could only be realised through knowing Jesus.

Wonderfully, Geoff saw what I was getting at and, a few weeks later, he repented of his sin and became a Christian. One of the things that helped him was to see that whereas freemasonry wanted to keep the 'most valuable knowledge' a secret from the uninitiated, God wants the most valuable knowledge of his Son to be spread to the ends of the earth. Anything worth having shouldn't be kept a secret! Geoff now wants everyone he meets to know about Jesus and he's even more passionate about the gospel than I am!

Sometimes you can get into the frame of mind where you want to 'season your conversation with salt' when you're not even talking about spiritual things, just to see what may happen! Standing at a bus stop once, I got talking to an elderly lady about (original, this) the weather! We remarked on how cold it was and how it would be great when summer came. 'Are you going anywhere on holiday this year?' I asked. She told me all about where she was going, then I said, 'I'm going to a Bible Week.' She could have just said, 'Oh, that's nice,' and finished the conversation there – that's a risk 'saltiness' must be prepared to take. In fact, we had a long chat about Jesus until her bus came.

If you've ever tasted a certain food that was utterly delicious then chances are you've tried to get your friends, workmates or even total strangers to try some of it too and enjoy the same gastronomic experience. If the gospel is utterly delicious to you, then finding ways in which you can introduce it to people around you will not be a repellent concept to you. Slipping a little salt into your speech is one way to do it. But remember, it's grace seasoned with salt – not salt seasoned with grace!

Where do we go from here?

1. Use Colossians 4:2–6 as a framework for your praying this week. Pray through each issue, e.g. being devoted to prayer, acknowledging the sovereignty of God, being watchful and thankful, praying for others who are seeking to draw people to Jesus etc.

2. Pray especially for yourself that God would give you wisdom in the way you relate to people, grace and salt in your speech, clarity when you are talking about the gospel and most importantly that he would 'open a door for our message'.

3. Write down some ways of communicating the following theological concepts in simple, jargon-free language: atonement, salvation, justification, sanctification. If you're not sure what some of them mean yourself, try some of the books listed at the end of this book.

19

Making the Most of Every Opportunity

We looked in the last chapter at ways of being effective at communicating the gospel to people. Now I want to share something that has helped me immeasurably to 'make the most of every opportunity'.

There are times when you can't have a long conversation with someone. Maybe their bus is coming or they're wanting to serve the next customer in the queue. You want to leave them with something that may spark off an interest in Jesus. What do you do? Give them your 'personal tract'.

There are lots of gospel tracts on the market, but the one I give out the most is the one I wrote! The reason is because it's personal: it's about me, and about what Jesus has done in *my* life, not in someone else's. It covers my view of Jesus before, during and after my conversion. It's a true story, and people love a true story. I remember giving one of my personal tracts to a lady in the street once. She stopped and read it there and then. When she had finished, she looked at me and said, 'That's a **** good read, that!' She was gripped by the fact that what she read had actually happened.

People may argue about your beliefs but they can't argue

with your story. I gave my tract to an elderly lady when I was
out shopping on one occasion. Years later, she came up to me
at a church meeting and told me how she had become a
Christian. She had read my tract and carried it around in her
handbag from the time I gave it to her. She would read it
every now and then as she took steps in her life closer and
closer to Jesus. She eventually became a Christian, but it was
years after I first met her. She still carries that tract around
with her and makes other people read it!

> ❝ People may argue about your beliefs but they
> can't argue with your story. ❞

The power of a personal tract is that it can speak about
Jesus long after you've gone, and sometimes to people you
never gave it to in the first place. I was out one evening doing
door-to-door visitation and at one house, I spoke to a man
who wasn't really interested in what I had to say. As he closed
the front door, I held out my personal tract to him. 'Can I
give you this?' I said. 'It's a leaflet I wrote about the most
amazing thing that's happened to me. Have a read!'

'OK, thanks,' he said, taking it. 'I'll read it over a cup of
tea.'

Before I got to the gate I thought to myself, 'I bet he
chucks it in the bin along with his teabag, without even
reading it.' (I found out later that that's exactly what he did!)

Later that evening, the man's daughter came down from
her bedroom to empty her ashtray. As she went to throw
away her fag-ends, she noticed my tract. Taking it out of the
bin, she went back upstairs and began to read it. A few days
later, I got a letter from her saying how she had found my

tract and that what she read had been very relevant to things she had been thinking about God. She asked to meet me to talk some more. My wife and I met her that Saturday and she came to church the following day, where she responded to the gospel and was born again. I couldn't believe it! I saw in that moment how powerful a personal tract can be, and I've carried them with me ever since.

There is, of course, a downside to these stories: I have carried them around more often than I've given them out! To stay motivated, we need constant encouragement. Even having great stories to tell doesn't help you get new ones. I know more people who have personal tracts lying unused in their coat-pockets than I care to think about.

> ❛ The tract could be just one link in the chain of their salvation. ❜

A link in the chain

The problem is that most of the time we never see what God does in a person's life through our tracts. People don't always get in touch. The tract could be just one link in the chain of their salvation. The fact that you may not see all that is achieved can make you feel sometimes that nothing was set in motion. That's when you stop doing what you've been doing. I gave out hundreds of tracts during the time I experienced the three stories I related here. I don't know what came of all those tracts but the exciting thing is knowing that something must have happened in some of the lives of the people I gave them to. And one day I'll find out!

Writing your personal tract

There are several types of personal tract. For example, you
could write the story of how you became a Christian;
you could write about a specific healing you experienced; you
could write a family tract about your family life together as
Christians; or you could write about a specific event that
brought home to you the truths of the gospel.

A few years ago, I travelled on the cross-channel ferry, *Herald
of Free Enterprise*, about a month before it capsized, claiming
the lives of almost a hundred people. Standing on the deck, I
discussed with a friend of mine how 'well built' and 'secure' the
boat was. I can remember saying to him, 'You could never
imagine a boat like this sinking.' I've spoken of this event on a
number of occasions when talking about the things we put our
security in, and how God is the only one in whom we can be
completely secure, even though we die. I've also often thought
it would be a good illustration to use for a personal tract.

In the end, of course, the choice as to which type of personal tract you go for is yours. Once you've decided, there are
a few principles to follow. As most people go for the story of
how they became a Christian, I'll concentrate on a framework for writing about this, though some of the principles
will work for the others as well.

There are four basic stages to your story.

1. Brief description of life before conversion

Include some information on areas such as:

— What did you think about Jesus before you became a
  Christian?

— How did Christianity figure in your life?

2. Your conversion experience

— What caused you to think more seriously about Jesus?
— What were the circumstances that led to your repentance?
— What happened when you prayed, asking God to forgive you?

3. Brief description of life since conversion

— How has your life changed? (Give some specifics that people who are not Christians can relate to, such as healing, answered prayer, etc.)

4. Concluding challenge

— Up to this point you have been speaking about how God challenged and changed *you*. To avoid people just saying, 'That's nice for you, but it's not for me,' you now need your reader to see that the same challenge applies to *them* and the same change can come to *them*.

❛ if what you have been saying is good news for you, then it is also good news for them. ❜

Remember, repentance is not a choice to be made, it's a command to be obeyed. One of the best ways of helping people to see this is through using Scripture. So you need to include some suitable verses which show your reader that if what you have been saying is good news for you, then it is also good news for them. Without some sort of gospel outline from Scripture, your tract is just a

nice little story about how you became a happier person.
With the gospel, it becomes a tool that can cut to the
heart.

The best way I have found to present the gospel is to weave
it through the story – and the good thing about writing the
'How I became a Christian' type of tract is that a gospel
outline slips easily into it.

Section 1   Include some of the points about the human condition: made to know him, cut off from him, deserving judgement, unable to save ourselves, etc. You want your reader to
see that they are in the same boat as you were. Think about
putting in one of these scriptures: Romans 3:23, 6:23.

Section 2   Mention God's love for us, his sending Jesus to
rescue us by his death and resurrection. Look at scriptures
like John 3:16; Romans 5:8–9; 1 Peter 3:18.

Section 3   Discuss the power of God to change people, to
set them free from sin and to help them live differently. Use
scriptures such as Romans 8:28, 35–39; 2 Corinthians 5:17.

Section 4   Be clear about God's call to them (e.g. Acts
17:30). Your reader may not have known much about Jesus
before they read your tract, but by the time they reach this
point, they should know enough to get their life right with
him. See also Romans 10:9–10.

Whatever kind of tract you go for, the gospel outline is the
part that everything else should hang from. Use your story
to illustrate its points.

Then comes the hard work of editing. If you only had 1,000 words to tell your whole story wrapped around the gospel outline, then you would choose your words carefully. You would think through exactly what you want to communicate and not waffle. You need to edit your tract down to a readable level. Remember you don't have to go into intricate details; just be clear on what you do say. By mentioning one or two points of the gospel in each of the four sections, you are putting in the right amount of salt to make a person thirsty. The aim of a tract is to stir up an interest so that the reader will seek further information. It doesn't have to take on the size of Billy Graham's autobiography to accomplish that!

Show your tract to someone who is gifted evangelistically so that they can give you constructive criticism. After writing a final draft, get it printed (or word-processed), pocket-size! A catchy title will make a reader want to find out what your tract is all about. A photo of yourself on the front can add a personal touch and reminds a reader of what the person who gave them the tract looks like. However, faces change, hair and teeth disappear, wrinkles and grey eyebrows appear – so, if you get loads of tracts printed with your photo on and then spend years giving them out, you may well stop looking like the person on the front! I know someone who had a photo of their bearded face on their tract, then a short time later, shaved the beard off, only to be left with about 975 tracts they no longer felt keen on giving away.

I would suggest you get about 200 printed. That's plenty to start with. You get more encouragement from seeing how quickly you give out 200 tracts than from watching a pile of a thousand hardly seem to go down. Once you've given away the first 200, get another 200 and go for it again.

Put a contact phone number or the address of your church on the back where people can get in touch with you. I don't put my home number on mine deliberately, as I want people to know I'm part of a church and I feel it is wiser that they contact me through the church.

Finally, form the habit of giving your tract away everywhere you go. Use it as a business card. When someone asks you for a number to get in touch with you, give them your tract and say something like, 'Here's where you can reach me – the number's on the back of this leaflet I wrote about the most amazing thing that's ever happened to me. Have a read, then when we next talk, you can tell me what you thought.'

Give your tract away at the supermarket checkout, the petrol station, the bus queue, the cashpoint queue, the restaurant, the pub . . . I even gave one to a man as he came out of a betting shop once and told him it contained a dead cert tip that he should stake everything he'd got on!

Who knows? One day someone may contact you asking to meet so that you could help them get their life right with God. Believe me, it does happen.

Where do we go from here?

1. Plan some time into this week when you will sit down and start writing your personal tract – even if it's just rough notes to begin with. Get your Christian friend to keep encouraging you to get it done and once it's done, to give it out. And you do the same for them!

2. Form the habit of giving away your tract once you've got it. Make yourself accountable to your Christian friend over it, and check they are giving theirs away too. Encourage one another. Remember: what's set in motion by your tract is often more than you personally see accomplished.

20

The Promise Is for You

After the resurrection Jesus told his disciples to stay in Jerusalem until they were 'baptised with the Holy Spirit'. He had already commanded them to 'go and make disciples of all nations', but he tells them here that before they go, there is something vital they need, to ensure they accomplish the task: 'you will receive power when the Holy Spirit comes on you; and you will be my witnesses in Jerusalem, and in all Judea and Samaria, and to the ends of the earth' (Acts 1:8).

> **The Holy Spirit was not given primarily to spice up our Sunday services but to empower us to spread the gospel among our neighbours**

Jesus returned to heaven in order to send his Holy Spirit to believers so that they would have his power to witness. The Holy Spirit was not given primarily to spice up our Sunday services or mid-week prayer meetings, but to empower us to spread the gospel among our neighbours, friends, relatives, town, city, nation and to the ends of the earth.

To be honest, I wouldn't want to even begin trying to fulfil the 'great commission' unless I was baptised in the Holy Spirit. The Holy Spirit desires to release God's measure of boldness, courage, confidence and strength into our lives so that we don't have to rely on our own measure. He wants to help you to put into practice all the principles that we have covered in this book, so that you will be all that God intends you to be and you'll have the joy of leading many people to Christ. More than this, he wants to bring us the power to fulfil what Jesus said in John chapter 14 verse 12: 'I tell you the truth, anyone who has faith in me will do what I have been doing. He will do even greater things than these, because I am going to the Father.' God's desire for you and me is that we can say along with the apostle Paul, 'Our gospel came to you not simply with words, but also with power, with the Holy Spirit and with deep conviction' (1 Thessalonians 1:5).

The result of the early Christians being filled with the Holy Spirit was that the gospel spread. People became Christians in their thousands. Amazing miracles were seen. Incredible hardships were endured. The kingdom of God spread across the known world. In our day, we need to know the power of the Holy Spirit if we are to fulfil our part in the great commission-gathering in the 'not-yet-Christians' in our generation.

If you are not baptised in the Holy Spirit, you need to be – and the wonderful thing is that you can be, because 'The promise is for you and your children and for all who are far off – for all whom the Lord our God will call' (Acts 2:39). When Peter stood up on the day of Pentecost and spoke these words, *you* were one of the far-off ones he was talking about. The Spirit of God was not given for the early Christians alone; he was given for all believers until the end of time. He is the gift of God available to every believer. He grows the fruit of Christian attitudes and behaviour in our lives and brings gifts of God's power to us (see Galatians 5:22–23 and 1 Corinthians 12:7–11). Both the 'fruit' and the 'gifts' are intended to help us and empower us as we seek to be 'unbelievably friendly' and lead people to Christ. Let's face it, if God is offering to give us such wonderful gifts, we would be utterly foolish to turn them down.

Receiving the Holy Spirit

If you're not baptised in the Holy Spirit, here's how you can be – *and* how you can pray for others to receive him too. After having the joy of praying with someone to become a Christian, you can experience further joy in praying for them to be baptised in the Holy Spirit. They don't have to wait until they are mature enough, or have to wait until they understand it all (see the story of Cornelius' household in Acts 10:44). I will often pray for people to be baptised in the Holy Spirit immediately after they have been born again, as this is often when they are most open to receive from God.

Obviously they need to have some understanding as to who the Holy Spirit is and why they need him in their lives, but they don't need to pass an 'A' level exam on baptism in the Spirit before it can happen for them. Before praying for someone to be baptised in the Holy Spirit, I show them two or three of the following verses that talk about the Holy Spirit, what he does and how to receive him (Acts 1:8, 2:1–4,

4:31, 8:14–17, 9:17–19, 10:44–48 and 19:6–7). I'll also point
out how in these accounts, the results of being filled with the
Spirit were often vocal (speaking in tongues, prophecy, prais-
ing). Then I turn to some words of Jesus: 'On the last and
greatest day of the Feast, Jesus stood and said in a loud
voice, "If anyone is thirsty, let him come to me and drink.
Whoever believes in me, as the Scripture has said, streams of
living water will flow from within him"' (John 7:37).

Jesus is speaking here about receiving the Holy Spirit. I
point out that he is saying that to receive the Holy Spirit we
must:

● **Be thirsty**   Thirst makes water more than desirable – it
  makes it a necessity! A thirsty person doesn't drink to
  be sociable. To receive the Holy Spirit, a person has to
  want what God is offering.
● **Recognise that Jesus is the source**   'Come to *me* and
  drink,' Jesus said. He is the only one who can give us the
  Holy Spirit and he must be the only source of our spiritual drinking from now on.
● **Be a clean glass**   No one pours expensive wine into a
  scum-covered, dirty glass – they pour it into a clean
  glass. To receive the Holy Spirit we must have repented
  and become Christians, allowing God to cleanse us
  from our sin. Then Jesus will be pleased to pour his
  Spirit into our lives.
● **Drink**   Psalm 81:10 says, 'Open wide your mouth and
  I will fill it.'

I look for faith in the person that they will receive what God
has promised and I try to build their faith and expectancy

through the various scriptures we've looked at. Then I ask God to come and fill them with his Spirit. When someone gives you a present, you thank them for it. So we start praying and thanking God for this gift of the Holy Spirit. He wants to give us this gift and we want to have it, so we don't have to twist God's arm to get it!

The Bible describes a number of different experiences people had when the Holy Spirit came to them. Some acted as though they were drunk, others broke out into praise, some prophesied, others had not much outward expression but a new depth of love for God and other people. One of the most common experiences was of people speaking the praises of God in languages they had never learnt. Paul's words in 1 Corinthians, that he 'would like all of you to speak in tongues' (14:5), would seem to suggest that this gift of the Holy Spirit is not only for 'special' Christians, but for all believers.

Speaking in tongues

Speaking in tongues is a form of prayer and praise. The Bible says that when we speak in tongues we speak not to people, but to God. The ability to speak praise to God in a language we have never learnt is a gift from the Holy Spirit to help us declare all that our spirit wants to express to our heavenly Father, without the limitation of our normal language. When we use our normal language, our mind controls the process. When we speak in tongues, we do not mentally understand what we say, but our spirit is expressing all that is in our heart in praise to God. Not all Christians speak in tongues and it is not a requirement or the only proof of having received the Holy Spirit, but for most people in the Bible, it was the most common accompaniment of encountering the Holy Spirit.

Speaking in tongues helps us in many ways. When we praise God, it helps us to express our worship *in spirit and in truth*. When we face difficult situations and don't know how to pray, it helps us to cry out to God constructively. It helps us when we pray for others, bringing a greater sense of God's presence into the situation. It encourages us and does our spirit good – or, to use the biblical word, it 'edifies' us. There are times in our lives when we face personal hardships which can drag us down. Speaking in tongues brings us spiritual encouragement and combats the depression that the devil would have us be hurt by. When we look at some of the hardships the apostle Paul endured, no wonder we find him saying, 'I thank God that I speak in tongues more than all of you' (1 Corinthians 14:18)!

Praying for others

When praying for someone to be baptised in the Holy Spirit, it is a good idea to have at least one other person praying who is already baptised in the Spirit. This brings confidence and faith to receive. As we pray, thanking God in English, I get the person I am praying with to ask Jesus to fill them with his Spirit and give them the ability to speak in tongues. Then after a few moments I tell everyone to stop speaking in any language that they know and start speaking out loud in tongues! That may sound strange, but it's how we begin.

A friend of mine uses a brilliant illustration to help people at this point. 'When you first get up in the morning and turn on the hot tap, cold water comes out to start with, but after a few seconds, it begins to flow hot. As you begin speaking in tongues, you may feel it is cold and clinical, made up even, but after a few moments, it flows and flows from your "innermost being" just like Jesus said it would.'

Ephesians 5:18 tells us to 'go on being filled', so I remind people that we need to seek God each day to be filled with his Spirit.

It should be evident whether a person has been baptised in the Holy Spirit. Even if there is little outward expression, the person themselves should be able to tell you if they know something has happened or not. Sometimes, if a person has not been filled with the Holy Spirit, they could have a sticking-point with one of the four points we looked at above (Thirst/Jesus as source/Clean life/Actively drinking). I have also sometimes found that if a person has drunk in their past from spiritual 'wells' that are not from God, they may have to pray and renounce their involvement in those activities. Then when they come again to ask for the Holy Spirit, they receive him almost immediately. You need to be tuned in to the Holy Spirit yourself, so that he can give you discernment while you are praying, and then you can help them more effectively with any sticking-points.

❛ The power in us is not for us, it's for those around us. ❜

After praying with someone to be baptised in the Holy Spirit, I often finish by reminding them that what God has given them is primarily for other people. He gives us new life and fills us with the power of his Holy Spirit so that we might be a living illustration to lost people around us that he is real and is in the business of transforming lives. 'You will receive power . . . and you will be my witnesses,' Jesus said to the first disciples, and the promise hasn't changed. The power in us is not for us, it's for those around us.

A few years ago, I went to hear Jackie Pullinger speak at a church in Bedford. She had seen multitudes of people set free from drug addiction in the walled city of Hong Kong and give their lives to Christ. She told us that it was after she had been baptised in the Holy Spirit and began to pray regularly in tongues that the dying people in the walled city started to get healed. Hardened gangsters broke down and opened their lives to Christ. And soon she 'lost count of the number of changed lives . . .' around her. When she understood that the promise of Acts 2:39 was for her too, she became more effective.

And the same can be true for you. The promise is for you too. God does not lie. You will receive power when the Holy Spirit comes on you: power to be his witness, power to do the things Jesus did, power to be powerfully, unbelievably friendly.

Where do we go from here?

1.   Are you baptised in the Holy Spirit? If not, find someone you know who is and ask them to pray with you. Go through the material in this chapter again so that you are aware of what baptism in the Spirit is about. Look through the Scripture references and let them build your faith. Remember the Holy Spirit is a gift to you from God – you don't have to twist his arm to get this gift. Then pray and be filled!

2. Do you speak in tongues? If not, do you see how helpful this can be? Don't let any British reserve rob you of something that God counts as a good thing. Next time you are in worship, ask Jesus to fill you afresh with his Spirit and give you the ability to praise him in tongues. Then praise him in any language you like – except one you know!

3. Familiarise yourself with the points on being filled with the Spirit so that, when you next have the opportunity to pray with someone for this, you will know what you're doing.

4. Have any of your unbelieving friends become believers yet? If not, keep the faith – but not to yourself! Keep praying too. If you have had the privilege of praying with someone to become a Christian, that's great! Why not go through this chapter with them and pray for them to be baptised in the Holy Spirit too!

5. Look back on some of the questions and activities of previous chapters. Do you need to 'refresh yourself' by repeating some of those activities? If so, decide which ones and work them back into your day.

21

Into the Unknown

My favourite sport is surfing. Not wind-surfing – that's for
people who like wobbling across a lake on a giant piece of
plastic, before running aground on a patch of pond weed!
But *real* surfing is an extreme sport! It's about cold seas, big
waves, trying not to drown, and stuff like that.

When I started to learn to surf, I would wade out into the
sea and get used to riding my board into shore on the 'foam'
(already broken waves). I got really good at this. I could get
to my feet quicker than most other people in the water and I
was enjoying myself!

Then I began to notice that the 'real' surfers (like my friend
Tom) would swim out past the breakers and catch the unbro-
ken waves. The sight of them, picked up by a huge wall of
water, accelerating down its face, 'carving' and 'shredding' as
they went, was both exhilarating and frightening at the same
time. The speed was ten times what I was experiencing and
the rides often ten times as long. The adrenaline rushed
rather than strolled through their veins. I had been enjoying
myself until I saw what they were doing. My three-second
rides became merely 'fun' when they had previously been

'awesome'. 'Awesome' was now waiting 'out there' where the real waves were – but 'out there' carried a whole new set of lessons that I would have to learn while being completely *out of my depth* . . .

The most awesome experiences and challenges in evangelism lie in unfamiliar waters: miracles; healings; the faith that moves mountains. As I read through the New Testament, a lot of what I see is not my experience – multitudes coming to Christ, amazing healings and miracles . . . I feel as if I'm watching the early church ride the big waves while I'm still standing on the beach! But if I want to be out there too, I've got to be prepared to get out of my depth and away from what I'm used to. To get 'out there', we have to leave the safety of confidence in our own abilities and experience, and that's not an easy thing to do. Out where the miracles are, I'm not confident in my ability, and I have no experience, so fear of failure, fear of getting into something I can't handle, and fear of the unknown, keeps me in the 'safety' of the familiar shallows.

> **The thing about fear is that it's really good at stopping people from doing things.**

Fear or faith?

The thing about fear is that it's really good at stopping people from doing things. The fear of being dragged out into the mid-Atlantic by a rip-current has stopped me on many occasions from paddling out to where the good surf is. The fear of flying (or rather, the fear of falling out of the sky at 1,000 mph) makes me think twice about going abroad on holiday. The fear of being laughed at has often stopped me from giving out my personal tract.

So many of the unbelievers I'm meeting now need a miracle to break into their lives. They're mentally ill, long-term drug addicts or elderly folk gripped by senility. I've got no clever ideas for reaching them. No 'How to . . .' book covers the situations I'm finding myself in. This is deep water stuff, and it scares me. The temptation is to stay where I'm safe, and fear holds me back from greater involvement.

When I'm surfing, and I find I'm getting scared of going right out, I thank God for my friend Tom. 'I just know that you're going to love it, if you go out there!' he tells me. And I know he's right. 'I'll paddle out with you,' he adds, and draws me away from the shore. He stays just in front as I follow him out. As we go, he keeps telling me, 'You're doing great, we're nearly there!' Then, when we reach the right place, he stays close at hand while we take it in turns to get to our feet on a wave and. . . wiggle about a bit before falling off!

I paddle out with Tom because I trust him. I feel more confident with him around. However, it's a confidence in his ability rather than in mine. I know he won't leave me if I get into difficulties, and I believe what he says about how much fun there is to be had out there among the big waves.

When you sense the Holy Spirit calling you to get involved in some aspect of evangelism that has been previously out of your depth, thank God that he has promised to go with you. If you follow him 'out', you can trust him not to leave you but to keep encouraging and empowering you. It's a trust based on his ability to do what is required rather than on yours. We will still face fear, almost every time we come across an out-of-our-depth experience, but if we know the Holy Spirit is the one calling us to follow him, and we choose to launch out in pursuit of God, then we won't be allowing fear to rob us of all that God has envisioned us with. And I believe we will find that 'we really do love it when we go out there'!

There will always come a moment of choice when we face fear. Will we let our fears keep us in the waist-deep experiences, or will we choose to act, in spite of fear, and follow God? It all boils down to who you trust, and what you put your faith in. What we need is faith in the promises of God, in the truth of what Jesus said in John chapter 14 verse 12: '. . . anyone who has faith in me will do what I have been doing. He will do even greater things than these, because I am going to the Father.' There have been times when the choice to believe the word of God in the face of fear and doubt made all the difference to my experience . . .

Launching out

My friend and I were visiting an elderly man who was dying of cancer. He spent most of his day breathing pure oxygen through a mask because his lungs were almost completely destroyed. From time to time he would cough uncontrollably. He had been a God-hater for all his eighty-plus years and now reaching him for Christ seemed an impossibility, especially as his mind had also gone. During each visit, he would drift in and out of conversation, lose track of what we were saying, and repeat things we had heard him say at least twenty times before. Where do you start, with someone like that?

I felt the Holy Spirit say, 'I just know you're going to love it, if you share the gospel with him!' I looked at the old man, but I was far from sure. His nurse was in the next room; what would *she* do if she came in and found me talking about sin, death, hell and stuff like that? I was faced with the choice. I decided to go for it.

As I started to speak to him about Jesus, something remarkable happened. He straightened up, his breathing got easier and he seemed to be totally in his right mind. I slowly went through the gospel with him and asked him if he'd understood what I'd been saying. 'Yes,' he replied.

'You are dying, Fred. Do you want to be right with God when you face him?' I asked. 'Yes, yes, I do,' he said.

I led him in a simple prayer of commitment to Jesus which he prayed aloud with me. Then, as we finished, he looked me right in the eye and, with tears on his cheeks, he said, 'Thank you.' As soon as he'd said this, he was back to his former state: his senility returned and his breathing was laboured. But there was something in the way he had said 'Thank you' that told me he had done business with God. I can't explain it, but I *saw* it in him. Two weeks later, he died and, I believe, went to an eternity with Christ.

On another occasion, at the end of a church meeting, a lady came up to me and asked for prayer. She had damaged a tendon in her wrist and had it encased in a surgical strap, which she was going to have to wear for at least six weeks. I started to pray my usual general prayer for healing, when I felt the Holy Spirit say, 'If you don't start asking me for the miraculous, you're never going to see it!'

I looked at her arm: the strap was pretty impressive, obviously built to deal with major damage, not just a slight strain!

What if I started 'commanding a healing' and nothing
happened? What would the poor lady say if her hopes were
dashed? The choice was there: play it safe and just ask God
to bless her, or go for the healing. I went for the healing.

'Ooh,' she cried, shaking her arm, 'the pain has gone, the
pain has gone.'

'Don't muck about,' I said.

'I'm not, it's really gone!' she replied.

The following week, at the church meeting, she came up to
me – minus the surgical strap – and gave me a piece of paper.
It was a copy of a page from her medical record. On it, her
doctor had written how 'after prayer' the pain had gone, the
strap could come off early and there was only a 'slight ten-
derness' to show anything had ever been wrong. That may
not seem as impressive as if the lady had been totally healed
at the moment we prayed, but it excited me and boosted my
faith to continue to pray for healing. I know it also made a
lot of difference to the lady concerned, whose arm didn't
have to stay strapped up for weeks.

Shortly after I became a Christian, some friends and I
were at a conference in Brighton. We prayed with a lady who,
six years earlier, had broken her neck in a car crash, leaving
her paralysed from the neck down. As we prayed, over three
evenings, I watched the vertebrae in her spine 'pop' and
'crunch' back into proper alignment. Then, on the third
evening, I held her hand as she got up out of her wheelchair,
and we walked together slowly around the main hall of the
centre. I was overwhelmed – I had never experienced anything like this before and I was even finding it hard to believe
my own eyes!

When she sat back down, the lady asked us what she

needed to do to become a Christian! She was not even a believer in Jesus, and had only come to the conference on the off-chance that she might find some help for her condition. I kept in touch with her for almost a year afterwards and she wrote back saying that each day she would walk a little bit further, slowly gaining the strength back in her muscles. She was also enjoying her new life with Jesus and going to a local church.

Miracles *do* happen!

My excursions 'out to where the impossible things happen' have been very few, but each one has been exhilarating. And I saw in each one of these experiences that the miraculous power of Jesus can come to people like us, even today – in fact, especially today!

These are my 'best' stories from nearly twenty years of being a Christian. How many more I could have had if I hadn't played it safe and stayed in the 'comfort zone', I don't know. But I do know that I missed out on more than I saw. Of course, there have also been numerous times when I did 'go for it' in prayer for people and nothing happened. The point is though that we won't see anything if we don't get out and risk it. Trying and drawing a blank is better than not trying in case we fail.

Whatever stage you are at in developing your evangelistic ability, there are always going to be times when you find the next step is out of your depth. Nervousness gives way to fear and suddenly you're faced with the choice. To go for it, or not? For you, being out of your depth could mean plucking up the courage to talk about what you've experienced of

God, when the opportunity arises. It could be writing a personal tract and giving it away to people. Or, it could be praying for someone who seems beyond help, and running the risk of being misunderstood and ridiculed.

> ❛ Being brave doesn't mean you know no fear;
> it means you don't stop in the face of fear. ❜

Whatever it is, remember that if the Holy Spirit is prompting you, he'll be with you when you act. Being brave doesn't mean you know no fear; it means you don't stop in the face of fear. I can understand why and how nerves and fear stop people from doing what they sense the Holy Spirit is prompting them to do. Often it seems daunting to step away from the shallows and into the unknown. When that happens, remember this: the one thing we *do* know about the unknown is that God is waiting out there for us to join him – and that can make it a little easier.

And finally . . .

I've tried, through this book, to give you some of the principles that have helped me to become more 'unbelievably friendly'. I'm sure these principles are all within your grasp. (I can be so confident because they've all been within my grasp!) I've written about things that have been part of my experience, and though these may seem unimpressive in places, and some of the lessons obvious, I think it could perhaps be more useful for helping you to win people to Christ than if you'd read a book on 'How to start a revival'!

We may never do what Billy Graham has done, but we can

know the same joy that he knows at personally seeing people become Christians – and there's no other joy like it. In the parable of the talents, the reward for faithfulness was to enter into the *joy* of the master (Matthew 25:14–23). It is Jesus' great joy to save sinners, and the joy of winning souls is his reward to those who are faithful in sowing. If we do not sow, we will not reap, but if we sow, 'we will reap a harvest if we do not give up' (Galatians 6:9).

If you:

● are faithful in using the mobility you already have, developing it through prayer and action,
● combine enthusiasm with wisdom, while making the most of every opportunity,
● are being filled with the empowering Holy Spirit and overcoming fear, to step into the unknown,

then it won't be long before you begin to enter into the same joy as your master.

And isn't this the point? That all we are doing and attempting to do now, in leading people to Christ, is working towards that day when we stand before his throne. Every seemingly insignificant conversation about Jesus, on a train or in a pub; every personal tract given instead of held back; every chance opportunity or act of kindness towards unbelievers, is aimed at multiplying the joy on that day – for them, for us, but most importantly, for him!

'Therefore go and make disciples of all nations . . . And surely I am with you always, to the very end of the age' (Matthew 28:19–20).

Further Recommended Reading

Here are some books which have inspired me over the years and helped to 'keep the gospel fires burning'!

1 Biographies and autobiographies

Arthur Blessit, *Arthur, A Pilgrim* (Blessit Publishing 1985).

Richard Collier, *The General Next to God* (Collins 1965).

Arnold Dalimore, *George Whitefield* (Banner of Truth 1970).

Danyun, *Lilies Among Thorns* (Sovereign World 1991).

George Dempster, *Finding Men for Christ* (Marshall Pickering 1935, 1985).

Elisabeth Elliot, *Shadow of the Almighty* (Hodder & Stoughton 1958; OM Publishing).

Elisabeth Elliot, *Through Gates of Splendour* (Hodder & Stoughton; OM Publishing).

F.T. Grossmith, *The Cross and the Swastika* (Word 1984).

William Martin, *Billy Graham* (Hutchinson 1991).

John Pollock, *John Wesley* (Lion 1992; Kingsway 2000).

John Pollock, *George Whitefield* (Lion 1986).

There are also several inspiring biographies of John Newton.

2 Books to create a love of the gospel

Walter Chantry, *Today's Gospel* (Banner of Truth 1970).

John Drane, *Jesus and the Four Gospels* (Lion 1979).

Nicky Gumbel, *Questions of Life* (Kingsway 1993).

R.B. Kuiper, *God-centred Evangelism* (Banner of Truth 1961).

D. Martyn Lloyd-Jones' series of expositions on the book of Romans (Banner of Truth).

D. Martyn Lloyd-Jones, *The Cross* (Kingsway 1986).

Rebecca Manley Pippert, *Out of the Saltshaker* (IVP 1979).

John Piper, *Let the Nations be Glad* (Baker, USA 1993; IVP 1994).

Laurence Singlehurst, *Sowing, Reaping, Keeping* (Crossway 1995).

C.H. Spurgeon, *The Soul-winner* (Eerdmans 1963).

Larry Tomczak, *Divine Appointments* (Servant 1986).

John Young, *The Case Against Christ* (Hodder & Stoughton).

Start

by Terry Virgo

You've made a start in the Christian life – where to now?

Should you be baptised? What about the Bible? Why is prayer important? Who is the Holy Spirit?

Whether you're a new Christian, or someone who simply wants to make a fresh start by getting back to the basics of your faith, you may be asking questions like these.

To help find the answers Terry Virgo presents thirty-one interactive studies so that you can build a firm foundation for your faith and future.

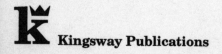

Kingsway Publications

unlcage key
Z K V k F E P bp A u g

ODS code
Y01922

Account
1585601L345

He careo4 m2G D.

Carol Bridget Gisele